Praise for *Finding*

"All too often we hear the false claims and empty promises of how to succeed in life and business offered by the latest 'fads of the week.' The time-tested methods presented in *Finding Personal Balance* allow each of us to truly understand that the answers and direction we are searching for come from within ourselves. I have been a strong advocate of the Choice Cycle in both my business and personal life for almost ten years now. The innovative concepts Will highlights in this book have been fundamental in helping me to quickly turn numerous struggling organizations into high performing teams, as well as to guide me through the daily ups and downs in my personal life. *Finding Personal Balance* is an essential guide that will influence how you approach every decision you make for the rest of your life."
Todd Sheppelman, Vice President, Visteon Corporation

"Will Ellis has been promoting and practicing the Choice Cycle Principles for many years. This book explains his teachings in an easy to understand way. Using his book, I have been able to share these ideas with subordinates and colleagues. It's really made a difference for me."
Michael J. Maloney, President, Global OEM, D&M Holdings

Finding Personal Balance

Finding Personal Balance

A Path to Inner Peace in a Life of Doing More

Will Ellis, Ph.D.

iUniverse, Inc.
New York Bloomington

Finding Personal Balance
A Path to Inner Peace in a Life of Doing More

Copyright © 2008 by Will Ellis, Ph.D.

iUniverse books may be ordered through booksellers or by contacting:

iUniverse
1663 Liberty Drive
Bloomington, IN 47403
www.iuniverse.com
1-800-Authors (1-800-288-4677)

Because of the dynamic nature of the Internet, any Web addresses or links contained in this book may have changed since publication and may no longer be valid.

ISBN: 978-0-595-47093-8 (pbk)
ISBN: 978-0-595-71760-6 (cloth)
ISBN: 978-0-595-91375-6 (ebk)

Printed in the United States of America

iUniverse rev. date: 11/11/08

To Shirley, the true source of balance in my life.

My deep appreciation goes to Susan Copeland, who inspired me to get started and supported me to the finish, and to Alma Muxlow and Dawn Dobson for their endless hours of help and attention to detail.

Contents

Introduction

Many years ago, my great-great-grandfather Charles Perkins Ellis and his wife, Sarah, left Springfield, Pennsylvania, for a new settlement just outside of present day Milwaukee. They were alone on the edge of a new frontier, plodding along at two miles per hour on worn Indian trails, never really sure what rounding the next bend would bring. Driven by hope for a fresh start in a new land, they followed the promise of a life of abundance. But the road was tough.

Thirty-year-old Charles and twenty-six-year-old Sarah made the trip from their Pennsylvania home in 1842. It wasn't all that long ago relative to our total history, but it was a world much different from today's.

Just a few years earlier, the Black Hawk Indian War had been fought practically in their new backyard. After the dust settled, pioneers began claiming eighty-acre parcels of land in and around Milwaukee. One of those parcels was granted to Charles and Sarah.[1]

I often reflect on what life was like for them, making that long trip in their horse-drawn wagon across the new America. The nearest doctor or medical support might have been a hundred miles away—or on the moon, for that matter. Food was scarce, and a decent dinner depended upon a successful hunt along the way. Fortunately, they traveled in a world of abundance, and the wilderness provided lots of leaves before the days of commercially available toilet paper! (The first factory-made paper marketed exclusively for toilet use was produced in the United States in 1857.)

Following their arrival on the new frontier, Charles and Sarah bore three children who lived past infancy, presumably delivered with the support of a midwife, far away from the comfort of immediate family. Charles hired help to build their log home from the trees on their new property, and of course there was no electricity or indoor plumbing. Their new house stood fourteen by sixteen feet, about the size of a nice master bedroom by today's standards.

Charles and Sarah shared their space with wayward travelers—on one occasion with fourteen teamsters—to earn extra money. It seems crazy now to be upset that my parents made me share my bedroom with two brothers!

A good growing season kept their family fed, but a lean harvest from the garden made it tough. They staved off the bitter Wisconsin winters with wood heat, but the mornings were chilly until the fire was rekindled.

Charles and Sarah couldn't catch the next day's weather on the Weather Channel or online, so they looked up at the stars instead and prayed for good weather for their crops. Prayer was an essential ingredient for getting through life in those days. Maybe it's the same now, but back then praying seemed so necessary.

Yes, life was difficult on the frontier in the 1840s. Of course we have our own share of stress and suffering in this fast-paced world. In a society driven by a global economy, demanding that we do more with less, it seems as if life gets harder all of the time. But does it? Is our life today really more difficult than the life faced by Charles and Sarah years ago?

Maybe life has always been difficult. I would guess that Charles thought that *his* great-great-grandfather Richard Ellis from Wales had a difficult life too.

Stories passed down through the family say that Richard's father had died in 1717 when Richard was only thirteen years old. That same year, Richard's mother put him on a ship from Wales to America so he could live there with an uncle, and upon his arrival in the New World, the ship's captain sold him into indentured servitude for seven years. Young Richard was a slave living on a brand-new continent at age thirteen. Now that's tough!

Struggling to cope with the stress of life is not new. We have traded physical stress for mental stress in a world driven by technology and characterized by speed, but there have always been challenges in life.

Some pundits in the 1950s predicted that our limbs would atrophy as technology provided for our every need. This hasn't happened yet, but we do live in a society that strives for instant gratification and instant results. Living in today's world is indeed stressful. We seem to be working more and more hours and our need to find balance in life has become acute. After twenty-eight years in a leadership coaching practice across a variety of organizations, I increasingly hear that people feel more stress, have too much to do, and enjoy their work and their lives less. At some level that's it, just simply enjoying life less. Peace of mind and joy seem so elusive.

That's the purpose of this book, to help any who are interested find a little more peace of mind and a little more fulfillment in their lives. In a world that gets smaller and spins faster, the increasingly difficult challenge is to enjoy the journey. Even if life always has been and always will be challenging, we have a *choice* in our experience.

CHAPTER 1

PERSONAL BALANCE
IS INSIDE

"There are dark moments in this struggle, but I want to tell
you that I've seen it over and over again, that so often the dark-
est hour is that hour that appears before the dawn of a new
fulfillment."

—Martin Luther King, January 25, 1965

Steelcase, the global office space manufacturer, financed a 1996
study to explore growing workplace trends in the United States.
One interesting finding was that twenty-three percent of office
workers spend at least some time during their vacations working.
A follow-up study conducted only nine years later revealed that
figure had jumped to forty-three percent! Nearly half of office
workers do some work on vacation, and only sixty-one percent
take all of their allotted vacation time. That's nearly two in five
people who do not take the time they have earned off work.

Another interesting discovery from the study was that the
"lunch hour" had shrunk to an average of thirty-six minutes, and
by 2005, the time had further dwindled to only thirty-one min-

utes. Nearly every time I tell this story to groups, the majority respond, "Who gets thirty-one minutes for lunch?!"

For those of us who remember the two-hour business lunch at a nice restaurant, punctuated by leisurely conversation, the good old days are gone. What ever happened to the three-martini lunch? No vacations, working on vacation, and turning our lunch hours into an optional lunch break are all symptoms of the race we are caught up in today.

It's not a surprise that the wealth accumulated in the West, especially in the United States, is being redistributed across the globe as other nations become educated, develop superior manufacturing capacity, and earn well-deserved investment from our capital markets. The side effects—such as no time—are what we didn't really predict.

After World War II, a good deal of Europe's and Japan's manufacturing capabilities had been decimated. Before China or other Asian-Pacific countries began their industrialization in earnest, manufacturers in the United States could produce as much as the workforce allowed and sell their products across the world. Perfect quality? Not always, but it was the only game in town. As everyone around the world grew in their ability to compete, the old way of doing things no longer worked.

In the West, where we *must* do more with less to compete, at least until we develop more proprietary products and technologies, we bought into a commonly accepted illusion that we would work forty-hour weeks, take four weeks of uninterrupted vacation time, and retire in our early fifties, with full pensions and lifetime medical benefits. We shared a commonly held belief that we were further ahead than our ancestors, more intelligent than our global neighbors, and entitled to those benefits.

This was just a delusion, what I call the "illusion of reasonable workload." The laws of nature have a way of reconciling our views with reality, sometimes rather painfully. Nature always wins, and our recent past is a temporary reality that we may never see again, certainly not in our lifetime.

Organizations that survive and thrive need their people to do more with less. We're simply not going back to our past.

No Settling. No Slowing.

Another illusion that permeates our organizational thinking is the "illusion of impending stability." We say: "As soon as things settle down around here, I am going to get back to normal. If I can only put in a few more hours this month, then hopefully next month will settle down." Ha! Life is not going to settle down for us, and there is no slowing it down. *Back to normal* is gone.

The challenge, then, is finding some kind of work-life balance in a world with more to do. The paradox is that we will be working harder and working more hours, so where is the balance in that?

The very phrase "work-life balance" can create an assumption that starts us down the wrong path. We believe we should work fewer hours and spend more time with our friends, families, or personal hobbies. After all, isn't that what work-life balance is all about? Isn't the goal to spend less time on activities that create stress and spend more time on the things that diminish stress?

This false assumption can lead us to believe our corporations are responsible for our balance. It is easy to assume that organizations—if they truly care about us—will provide balance by lowering their expectations of us, or at least by scooting us out the door at a reasonable hour so we spend less time at work. We expect our institutions to hire more people and to more equitably spread the work so we can leave for the day at a civil time. We want to place the responsibility for our balance on our employers, or at least on our managers.

Organizations that *truly* care about their employees will survive and grow, so we continue to have jobs in this more competitive world. They will ask more from us. And not just to work harder and faster and longer, but also to find ways to work smarter. Maybe for a time, though, we will need to work harder and faster and longer, too. Global competition, new technology, new processes, and cost reductions that sometimes include staff cutbacks are real factors that will require us to do more. Good ideas are not always born between 9 AM and 5 PM, and next year we will have to do *more* all over again.

Those who work for the highest performing organizations work hard. Many of these organizations are also rated the best places to work and provide benefits like flexible work hours, day care services, and financial benefit options that build employee loyalty and offer solutions to the problems of workload stress. These benefits allow employees with demanding outside needs the chance to get it all done.

The best companies to work for may even provide in-house recreational facilities and meditation rooms so employees get a refreshing break from the grind. But if we wait for our establishments to provide us with balance in our lives, we'll follow failure with disappointment. "One of these days I need to find more balance ..." Remember the illusion of "impending stability?"

We need to take back the responsibility for our lives and be thankful if we work for organizations who ask a lot of us. We may find process improvements, but work is infinite, and we will always have more to do. As Seth Godin, author, entrepreneur, and agent of change says, "The problem with infinity is that there's too much of it." So how can we break the cycle of more work and more pressure and more stress?

We need a new way of thinking about balance. One way to find *personal balance*, not work-life balance. The goal of personal balance is to find a sense of peace in a world of stress and change. After all, the outcomes most of us really want are peace of mind, a sense of calm, and more joy in our lives. We long to become centered.

We can get all of those things even if we need to work more. The best part is that personal balance is something we can always find within ourselves, no matter what circumstances are around us. We don't need to look to others. We can take the responsibility back where it belongs—within ourselves. Personal balance is already there, inside of us, always ready for us to rediscover.

Personal balance is about doing the things we already know, to become the people that we already are.

When we look inside ourselves, we discover wisdom that is embedded from generations of repeated human experience. We have a prime example, or archetype, for finding peace in our lives, no matter the current chaos around us. We have the wisdom to find the balance that is already there, deep inside.

Leaders in Service

Our perspectives are relative. A workshop I have conducted for several years includes a day of community service, completed together in work teams. I call the program "Leaders in Service" and follow the day of service with exercises and dialogue designed to help participants bring the lessons from their experience back to their workplace. These lessons are: the power of teamwork, the emergence of leadership from everyone, and the inherent value of being in service to others.

One consistent lesson from "Leaders in Service" is that our problems lose their hold on us when we change our perspectives. Think differently about the world around us and our problems evaporate. If one works on a Habitat for Humanity home for someone who cannot afford decent housing, even the most modest home with a warm bed feels especially welcoming at the end of the day. If one delivers food to homebound seniors who don't have enough to eat, a simple meal at the end of the day with family becomes a bountiful harvest. If someone takes a group of children from a homeless shelter for a tour of a hands-on museum, he quickly realizes that if not for "the grace of God," those children could be his own.

"Leaders in Service" is a powerful experience for employees of organizations where, for a myriad of reasons, morale is not high. A change in mindset emerges: How we feel about our current circumstances is a reflection of the way we choose to think about the world around us. Our problems are not big when compared to the difficulties experienced by others and to those of the generations who preceded us.

We create our own hardships, and they are largely ours by choice. One ingredient for finding balance is keeping life in perspective. And that is the central theme of this book. If we want to find personal balance, we have the power to choose it. It is always there, waiting inside, and we can call it forward.

CHAPTER 2

START WITH A CHOICE

"The real voyage of discovery consists not in seeking new landscapes, but in having new eyes."

—Marcel Proust

Anyone who has achieved personal balance finds a way, at some point, to walk out the door and go home. Because work is infinite, most of us could work as much as we want. But leaders in the best companies create visions that inspire us to do even more, not less. A quick walk through the corridors of the most respected organizations paints a picture of intense focus and effort, not the relaxed atmosphere of a country club.

The reality is that our work is *not* going to slow down, and if we suffer from the illusion of impending stability, the idea that things will settle down soon, we will be sadly disappointed and probably blame our employers. If we want to find personal balance in our lives, we need to start by choosing personal accountability. Speaking with honesty and conviction, our mantra has to become, "I am responsible for balance in my life!"

Can you honestly say that to yourself today? When we blame others or anything outside of ourselves, we are doomed to continue a negative cycle of imbalance in our lives. Change starts by facing the cold hard truth inside of ourselves, not outside.

Everything Is Perfect

In some way, all of us are trying to get better outcomes at work and in life.

When I ask the question, "What outcomes *should* you be getting right now?" most will give answers describing the results that they would *like*. On the personal side, most say they want to enjoy the journey a little more, have less stress, more sleep, more time with family—in general, time to smell the flowers. When it comes to work, they say they would like higher quality, better customer satisfaction, higher productivity, more pay and bonuses. But all of these are answers to the question, "What outcomes would you *like* to get right now?" not "What outcomes *should* you be getting?"

There is only one answer to the "should" question—exactly the outcomes that you ARE getting.[2] Fortunately for us, the world operates in orderly ways, governed by the principles of physics and the laws of science. As far as we know, the universe is a lawful place where certain actions predictably create certain reactions or results.[3]

Every effect has a cause, whether we can observe and understand it or not. Every result in our lives is caused by some preceding action or force, or in other words, everything happens for a reason. Every outcome we experience, from our emotions (how we feel) to our accomplishments (our failures and our successes), happens for a reason.

In other words, all our results are perfect. Though often not what we would prefer, our results are a perfect outcome of the factors present to create them. This principle is freeing to know. The world is not just a random place. And the implication is that we have a chance to understand how we get certain results and, more importantly, how to create different results.

For example, I like to proclaim to others that the weather is always perfect. During the winter months in the North and the summer months in the South, some tend to scoff at this notion, "You have got to be kidding me!"

But think about it. Look outside right now. What is causing the weather you are seeing out your window? Factors affecting your weather are the natural conditions that cause *exactly* the weather you are experiencing. Those conditions include atmospheric conditions, your location in the northern or the southern hemisphere, the barometric pressure, the position of the moon and other planets, the tilt of the earth, your distance from the sun, the current conditions on the sun, the amount of greenhouse gasses in the atmosphere, and so on. Our weather is a perfect result of all the conditions present to create it. So, I contend, the weather *is* always perfect!

Now, the weather is not always what we want it to be, but it is always perfect. And, like many other phenomena we experience in our lives, we don't control the weather, but we can do many things to change our experience of the weather. We could, for instance, move to a more favorable climate or we could use a fan or even install an air conditioner.

...

"All of us could take a lesson from the weather.
It pays no attention to criticism."
- Anonymous

...

The imperfection is our expectation of how the universe should act. *The problem is in us!* As human beings, we are masters at rationalizing the world around us, but the results we get are always perfect.

There is no silver bullet that is going to make us balanced, happy, wealthy, or famous overnight, and this should not surprise us. We don't really control all of the outcomes we get, but we do influence them, and successful people find ways to increase their influence.

The power in thinking differently about the world is that doing so creates different results. If we spend our energy focusing on the results we want instead of moaning and groaning about our problems, we stand a better chance of creating something different.

A Choice We Make

How do we create different results? We have to *do* something different—take some action. Our influence is strengthened through action and our only chance is to *do something*, even though there are no guarantees that we will get exactly what we want.

We have the power to create different outcomes by choosing how we respond to the world around us. Taking different action starts with first choosing how we view the world.

What are the factors that cause a certain response in us? We tend to assign motive to things that happen to us. After a miserable day, frazzled to the core, someone might say, "Wow, you look like you've had a tough day. What happened to you?" We instinctively respond, "Those customers have impossible demands!" or "My boss was in a bad mood today—he yelled at everyone in his path!" or maybe even, "The traffic was crazy out there—those other drivers are idiots!"

Winston Churchill was quoted as saying: "History is just one darn thing after another!" I think he was right. And we explain our actions through the prism of these life events. We draw the explanations for both our behavior and our emotions from the events around us. Things happen *to us*, and they *cause us* to react in a certain way. "That driver cut me off right in the middle of rush hour traffic! I am so stressed out!"

Things do happen to us in our lives, but it's the belief in the causal connection that robs us of our capacity to make a difference in our results.

We don't always choose what goes on in our lives, such as those other drivers, but we do have a choice about how we react and feel, which may be our only true choice in life.

The Last Freedom

Viktor Frankl elegantly makes this fundamental point in his landmark book, *Man's Search for Meaning*. Dr. Frankl tells a riveting story about his experiences in Nazi concentration camps during World War II. As an Austrian psychiatrist and a Jew, he was rounded up with many others who were moved in railroad cars to the camps for grueling work details or, worse, extermination. Frankl's story is not about the heroes within the camps but the nameless, faceless multitudes who suffered through the worst experience possible.[4]

Dr. Frankl couldn't have lost much more through his ordeal. His parents were killed, his wife died alone in a separate camp, and his children were taken away from him. Only one daughter lived through the horror.

Those who survived were subjected to the worst imaginable living conditions, if one can call that living. Perhaps the most horrible part was the total loss of human dignity. The prisoners' basic human rights and freedoms were stripped away, all under a cloud of intense fear for one's life, as inmates were randomly murdered at the whim of the guards or the capos. Their suffering is difficult to imagine.

Viktor Frankl became interested in the resilience of the souls who survived, despite their hardships. He observed that some simply gave up as the pain became too much for them. Frankl could tell when a fellow prisoner had surrendered hope, because he would see the man smoke his own cigarettes.

In a Nazi concentration camp, cigarettes were used as a currency or a form of barter. A prisoner could trade a cigarette with a guard for a pair of shoes, so he wouldn't have to work barefoot in the snow during his work detail. Maybe a cigarette would buy a little piece of meat in his soup that night, giving him the energy to continue the struggle.

When someone began to smoke his own cigarettes, it was clear that "he had given up faith in his strength to carry on, and, once lost, the will to live seldom returned." Everyone knew the signs. In a few days, the prisoner would die.

Some, on the other hand, found ways to survive. Viktor Frankl was struck by the concept of the *last freedom*; that is, as human beings, our last freedom is to always choose our attitude, our mindset, how we feel, and what we think, no matter the circumstance.

Frankl captures the message poignantly: "We who lived in concentration camps can remember the men who walked through the huts comforting others, giving away their last piece of bread. They may have been few in number, but they offer sufficient proof that everything can be taken from a man but one thing: the last of the human freedoms—to choose one's attitude in any given set of circumstances, to choose one's own way."[5]

One point that becomes clear from Viktor Frankl's story is that if he could survive life in a Nazi concentration camp, then what do we have to worry about? Our perspectives are always relative.

When we accept the notion of the last freedom, life's negative events lose their power over us. No matter what happens to us, the choice remains inside us, not outside in the world of events around us. The other drivers on the road, no matter how crazy, lose their power to stress us out. The weather, no matter how different from our ideal, cannot make us feel miserable. The autocratic boss, no matter how insensitive, will never negatively affect our performance.

We have only limited influence on whether or not life brings us challenges and obstacles, but we have almost unlimited ability to cope with them. "Life has suffering" is the first noble truth of Buddhism and a truism that we catch onto pretty early in life. Whether we like it or not, that's what life brings. It is a guaranteed part of being alive.

If you go through life expecting grief, what do you think you will get? Yes, grief! However, if you expect respect and appreciation, what do you think you will get? Now this is where life likes to throw us a curve, because no matter what, you will still get grief! That's the way life is. The point is that we don't always control the events in our lives; our only choice is in our response.

Mindsets

So, if the events in our lives do not cause our feelings and actions, what does? I propose that there are "filters" between whatever is going on in our lives and the actions we take, the most critical being our thinking, what I call our mindsets.

Our mindsets, or assumptions about reality, have been called by many names. Thomas Kuhn used the word "paradigms" to describe shifts in our scientific thinking.[6] This word was popularized in recent years by Joel Barker.[7] Peter Senge referred to our mindsets as "mental models."[8] Scott Peck professed that "our view of reality is like a map with which to negotiate the terrain of life."[9] Explaining his view of how we create the results in our lives, Larry Wilson called them our "mental maps."[10]

However we describe thinking patterns, our mindsets help us make sense of the world, navigate our way through it, and protect us from danger. Mindsets could also be described as our beliefs or our assumptions about how the world operates. Not necessarily religious thinking, but beliefs about the world we see and experience. Developed through our life experiences, mindsets are ways to understand and predict patterns in the world. We have mindsets for everything we perceive around us.

We use our mindsets to overlay meaning onto our life events. They fit the events into our worldview and make sense of it for us. Mindsets are neither good nor bad, they just are. We need them to frame the world around us and to help us respond in meaningful and appropriate ways.

...

"The meaning that we give an event is the event."
- Deepak Chopra

...

One purpose of mindsets is survival of the species. When any event happens, our mental maps help us decide what it means. We are not descendants of the branch of the human tree that came upon a saber-tooth tiger in the forest and said, "Oh, what a cute little kitty!" That branch was lopped off a long time ago! We are surviving as a species because of our ability to create mindsets about the world around us and to predict what might happen.

CHAPTER 3

THE CHOICE CYCLE

"Do or do not. There is no try."

—Yoda

My Diet

Losing weight and getting in shape are challenges many of us can relate to. Let's say, for instance, that I need to lose ten pounds. Okay, fine, twenty pounds. Unfortunately, I have lots of good reasons why I am not in perfect shape. If you ever come to one of my family reunions, you will find that everyone there looks exactly like me. So it's not really my fault. It's my parents' fault!

Heard this story before? In truth, everyone knows what to do—eat a healthy diet and exercise regularly. Oh my, how the truth hurts.

I don't know if your past diets look like mine, but I typically commit to start on Monday, because we all know that you can't start on the weekend, right? If it's Saturday night, I might as well live it up before I have to start my diet. Only two more days of fun to go!

My plan is to get up on Monday at 4:30 AM to exercise, probably jog, but I'll wait to decide on the specific kind of exercise when I get up on Monday morning. Then I am going to have a healthy breakfast, because as we all know, breakfast is the most important meal of the day.

You know what am I going to do when that alarm goes off at 4:30 AM on Monday morning, don't you? Boom! I reach over and slam that snooze button! Of course this is a reasonable response, because Monday is a tough day. So, I commit to start my new, healthier lifestyle the next day. Tomorrow! That's my new slogan. Nonetheless, I have a healthy breakfast: shredded wheat with no sugar, skim milk, and one piece of dry toast.

When I get to work, you know how I am feeling. Yes—hungry! But I am committed, so for lunch I have a healthy tossed green salad with low cal dressing on the side and some ice water. Just as I am finishing my salad, my friend walks into the cafeteria with a huge brownie. Not just a regular brownie, but one with walnuts and a big scoop of vanilla ice cream on top.

What do I say to myself about the brownie? Of course, I deserve it! After all, I have been good all day, and, anyway, what am I going to do tomorrow morning at 4:30 AM? Go jogging!! Yes—that is exactly right.

So, I *inhale* the brownie. By dinnertime, because my diet is blown for the day anyway, I eat a whole pizza. After all, I did have to work late, and so I deserve it. Somewhere in heaven, God is surely keeping track of all of my extra effort in life, and I am sure He would agree that I deserve treats to compensate for the difficult life I lead.

One of the treats I deserve is dessert. It has been a long day. One scoop of rocky road is not nearly enough, so I proceed to get frost freeze on my face eating ice cream directly out of the freezer. Everyone knows that little bites taken directly from the refrigerator don't have many calories. In the end, I am well on my way to gaining another ten pounds![11]

What are the lessons behind this story? First, our actions combined with other factors (in this case, a principle of energy consumption: *calories consumed minus calories spent equals weight gain*) create exactly the outcomes we get. All the results that exist in the universe, whether outcomes or our emotions, *are perfect*. In fact, even though we sometimes don't like it, the universe remains a perfect place.

Secondly, we constantly make choices regarding both how we think and the actions we take to get exactly the results we experience. Genetics and other uncontrolled conditions make a difference, certainly, but we still make choices that create the outcomes. **We have choices**.

The Choice Cycle represents the experience of life's events—whatever is going on in our lives—and the way these are filtered through our mindsets. This triggers our actions, which then influence the outcomes we get. Finally, those outcomes, including our results and our emotions, go on to influence our future life events.

The Choice Cycle

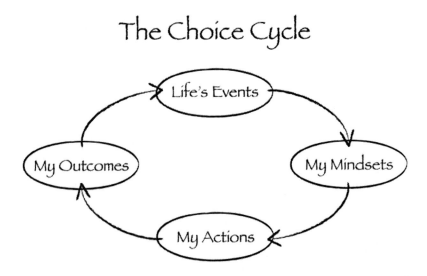

Insanity has been described as doing the same thing over and over, expecting different results. We don't always control the results we get, but if we want different results, such as achieving more success or experiencing more positive emotions, we know that we need to *do* something different.

Success isn't about waiting for the world around us to change, but taking action to create more successful outcomes. And if we expect to change our behavior, we had better start with the way we think about the world around us—our mindsets. The first step toward improved results is thinking differently—more effectively—about life's events.

What Are My Stories?

Another way to look at mindsets is that they are the stories we tell ourselves about life. A story is the meaning we attach to observable data to make sense of it and fit it into our framework for the world around us. Stories are not necessarily right or wrong. Stories are simply a way to interpret what we see, hear, touch, smell, or taste.

As human beings, we often use stories to explain away events that are difficult to understand or that put us out of our comfort zones. We accept seemingly rational stories from one another every day masking a more honest, underlying motivation for our actions.

> "I don't have time to work out right now. I've got too much to do."
>
> "I didn't have time to call you back."
>
> "I am going to start my diet on Monday."
>
> "I have been working hard and I deserve to treat myself."
>
> "I am entitled to certain privileges in life."
>
> "I wasn't born to work with people. I am too shy."
>
> "The reason I became an engineer is that I like to work with facts. I am no good with customers."
>
> "The reason I work in sales is that I like to work with people. I am no good with numbers."
>
> "I didn't mean to get into debt, it just happened. What could I do?"

The surprising thing is we accept these stories from each other and from ourselves. We've all heard these stories and many like them, and we tend to support one another in these delusions. "It's okay—Monday is the toughest day of the week!"

We are part of an evolving culture that avoids accepting personal accountability for our actions and for the outcomes we create. It's much easier to support each other in blaming the world around us and being victims in our thinking, rather than challenging each other to be survivors.

Stories are not always false rationales, but can be good ways to understand the present and to predict the future. The world teaches us time and again, however, that stories we firmly hold onto need to change as the world around us changes.

One ingredient of success in any venture is to keep a "beginner's mind," to always be open to new perspectives. Psychotherapy is a process of discovering old mindsets and stories we cling to that no longer serve us. These mindsets block us from creating the results we really want.

...

"In the beginner's mind, there are many possibilities;
in the expert's, there are few."
-Shunru Suzuki

...

In reality, the world is full of random events that occur out of our control. While we do not control the events in our lives, how we respond to those events—starting with how we think about the world—is within our control.

Driving

We often color what is going on in our lives with our own personal stories and mindsets about how we believe the world *should* work. Driving is an experience most of us share, and it often is a frustration we allow to get the best of us. It also provides great examples of the way our mindsets work.

Today's abundance of road rage incidents indicates something about the driving stories we tell ourselves and the common "truths" that emerge. Some drivers believe that they are teaching their fellow drivers a lesson when they lose their tempers and lash out. "How will they ever learn if I don't teach them?" Are we as a culture creating commonly held stories that add aggression to our lives? As we mature, we realize that we have a choice about the ways we react in traffic. *And we always get exactly what we choose!*

Have you ever been driving home from a tough day at work and had someone cut right in front of you, then veer off toward the exit? What did you think to yourself, or even possibly think out loud? (I know, it isn't fit to print here.) All of us can tell stories about the idiots out there on the road.

Instead of reacting in anger, consider another point of view. You are driving home from a tough day at work, still thinking about the challenges from the day, when suddenly you realize your exit is *here*! You aren't even in the right lane! You see an opening in the right-hand lane and go for it. Uh-oh, the driver you accidentally cut off had to brake to avoid clipping your bumper.

You feel awful about almost causing a serious accident. Hopefully the other driver understands you are a fallible human being. You didn't intend to cut anyone off, and you are apologetic. Your hand signals the message, "Oh please—*I am sorry!*"

What is the difference in the two scenarios? In the first, someone cuts you off. In the second, you accidentally cut someone else off. How do you think and feel about each event? The difference is not the event, but how you react, think, and feel about it. In the first scenario, you are upset, stressed out, and ready to go home and scream at someone. In the second, you remain calm. Being cut off on the highway doesn't get us upset, it's our reaction that sets us off.

On days we choose to scream through the windshield at all of those "idiot" drivers, to get upset at every delay, to get angry with those who drive too fast or too slow (pick your favorite gripe!), we go home and yell at the dog, bark at the kids, get grumpy with our significant other, speed eat ourselves to indigestion, and lose sleep. On the days we choose to kick back and say to ourselves, "I might as well enjoy whatever life brings today," the dog, the cat, the kids—everyone—is a lot happier to see us, and frankly, we are a lot happier with ourselves.

Mind-Body-Spirit

The Choice Cycle focuses on the power of the human mind, the power of our mindsets, in choosing our attitudes. Our physical and spiritual states also influence how we frame events around us. The mind-body-spirit connection is real, and being healthy physically and spiritually can be just as important as being healthy mentally. Maintaining a positive mindset is difficult when our health is compromised in any of these areas, and healing from the events our past has dealt us requires a look at all three elements.

Simply feeling good physically can have a lot to do with how we interpret an event. Upon finishing a rigorous aerobic workout, big problems tend to melt into tiny aggravations. When someone is clinically depressed, everything can look discouraging and hopeless. A person with a hangover from the night before has much less capacity to handle even little annoyances. So there is a physiological component that must be considered.

We have varied definitions of the word *spiritual*, and many of us have strong beliefs that make discussions about spiritual growth sensitive. My point is not to land on the side of any one belief system or dogma, but simply to acknowledge that, at some level, we are spiritual beings in physical bodies. The health of the whole person cannot be ignored, and those with rich spiritual lives often cope more effectively with challenging life events.

The Choice Cycle

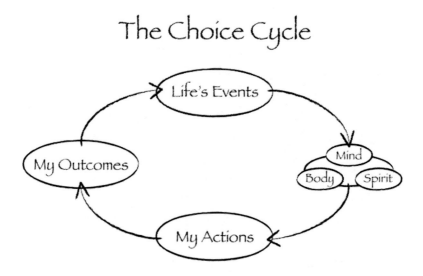

I will explore the mind-body-spirit connection further in Chapter 4, in the context of finding personal balance, but for now I want to focus on the power of the human mind.

No matter what is going on in our lives physically or spiritually, having the right mindsets about the world around us is a critical factor in creating the life outcomes we want. As Viktor Frankl taught us, no matter what else is going on in our lives, this is our last freedom.

If we are not getting the results we want out of life, what options do we have? We can accept the results we get, or we can behave in a different way to produce different results. The difference here is **personal accountability**—we are the only ones responsible for the results we get. This is not about the world around us—it is all about *us* and what goes on inside of us!

Mindsets are not inherently good or bad, but how do we know if we are holding onto a mindset or a story that is not useful? My contention is simple: We can determine that our mindsets are not working for us when we are not getting the outcomes we want. One example is when we are consistently feeling negative emotions like anger, frustration, anxiety, or sorrow. We tend to look outside of ourselves for reasons to explain why we don't get what we want. We want to blame someone or something. The key to getting different results, however, is to accept our lessons in life, look inside ourselves and ask, "What can I do differently to get different results?"

I don't want to gloss over the very real effects of true grief. Following the loss of a close loved one like a child, for example, we don't have a choice about the grief that follows, no matter what we say to ourselves. And frankly, we wouldn't want to. Grief is a natural reaction and a good one. It gives us time to cope with our loss, to reserve our energy, and to rest. Our mindsets may need revision, however, if we remain stuck in grief for years and we struggle to move ahead with living.

The key message of the Choice Cycle is this: "I am the only one who can create different outcomes!" We can wait for the world to change around us, but it may not. Personal accountability for the outcomes we create in our lives is not just a theory but a principle in nature. In the long run, nature always wins.

There is only one answer to the question, "Who is responsible for getting the results I want?" That answer is *I am!*

A journey to find personal balance always starts with acceptance of personal accountability. For every result that you want in your life, there is a way of thinking and acting that will give you that result. The key is being adaptable enough to let go of old thinking and to accept the ways and ideas that will make you successful.

CHAPTER 4

THE PATHS OF CHOICE

"It's not the mountain we conquer, but ourselves."

—Sir Edmund Hillary

What Life Brings

In the spring of 1970, I attended an anti-Vietnam War protest at Michigan State University in East Lansing. I had several friends who fought for their country in the Vietnam War, and, while I supported all of our soldiers, I wanted to get them back home, quickly and safely. Upon honest reflection, I was there for my beliefs, but also for the social event with some friends who were students at MSU.

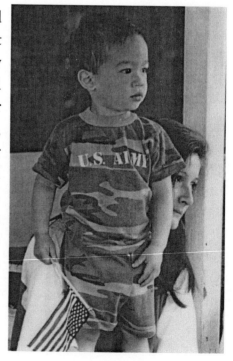

Based upon your own mindsets, I was somewhere on the continuum from traitor and outside agitator to a socially conscious soul expressing my disapproval of an unjust war. In any case, I was a peaceful demonstrator.

Anyone who has attended an event with thousands of people, whether a political gathering or a sporting event, has felt the energy of a large crowd speaking with a single voice, shouting in unison and with passion. The air was electric on that spring day as we walked peacefully down Grand River Avenue toward the State Capitol building in Lansing, chanting our slogans with conviction. The demonstration seemed well-planned, and some of the traffic lanes had been barricaded to ensure our safety. Our progress toward our destination was smooth on that glorious, sunny day, and it seemed like we could have changed the whole world, right then and there.

As the march progressed the sun began to warm us up, and by the time we were approaching the Capitol the weather was becoming hot and humid. We continued down Grand River Avenue past a long line of cars, bumper-to-bumper, facing us. Some of us spilled over the barricades and congested the streets. It took time for a few thousand people to walk by.

Some of the drivers who were sitting in their hot cars in standstill traffic were not inspired by our mission to stop the war. Especially those drivers who didn't view air conditioning as a critical need in Michigan. One could imagine that they didn't leave their houses to drive somewhere expecting to be delayed by a long parade of *communist-loving, rabble-rousing, hippie* antiwar demonstrators. Those who remember the time can recall the polarization that ripped a chasm between those with opposing political and social views, as a radically different generation expressed its values.

Fueled by a lethal combination of a long wait in the hot sun, hate-filled beliefs, and possibly some liquid courage, one driver decided he had had enough and began weaving his way through the middle of the demonstrators. The marchers didn't part for the driver as he expected, however, and he bumped one person, then another. He must have panicked then, because he suddenly, unbelievingly, accelerated, plowing through the middle of the crowd. A collective scream of horror and disbelief rose into the sky.

I had never before and have never since seen such chaos and confusion burst from a crowd. Some of the protesters were still caught in the fun and laughter that was everywhere only seconds before. Others watched but were immobilized by disbelief, plunged into a new reality they did not yet comprehend. Still others saw the situation unfolding before them but still were frozen in their tracks, unsure of the best response, disbelieving that this surrealistic moment would affect them. A few reflexively moved out of the way, but many did not have a chance.

As the car moved toward us, I remember pushing my girlfriend out of the way, as much an act of panic as anything heroic. The car careened by, just a few feet to my left, a close call. I will never forget the young people falling as the car struck them, crushing them beneath its tires. At that moment they were doomed to accept whatever the cruelest side of life dealt them. And I will never forget the sight of those kids—twenty-year-olds like me—being dragged underneath the car as it seemed to drive on forever and even further still, scraping skin off onto pavement. *Oh stop, please stop, please stop, please stop …*

For some merciful reason, that car finally stopped. The crowd swarmed the driver instantly, while I watched, still in disbelief. Just as he was being dragged from the driver's seat, the police came and took the driver from the hands of the mob, surely saving his life.

My friends and I immediately turned back for home, in shock, traumatized, barely able to speak about what we had seen that day. The rumors that spread afterward said that two people had died and several more were critically injured, although I have never been able to verify any of this information.

My friends who fought for their country and for each other in Vietnam lived through much worse, and it would dishonor their experience for me to claim that my ordeal on that spring day compared in any way with theirs. But anyone who has found themselves in the center of a panicking crowd, fought in a war, suddenly lost a loved one, been the victim of a crime, been in a serious automobile accident, or survived any of the many other traumatic experiences life brings our way knows that these events have an effect on us. At some point, after a normal grief response, we make a choice about how that life event will affect the rest of our time on earth.

What We Choose to Hold Onto

Difficult life experiences have a true, harmful effect if we choose to hold onto a negative outlook on life. If we choose to distrust other people, we lose as a result. If we see danger and harm all around us, we miss a lot of joy. If we begin to fear and to avoid risk, life won't hold the same spark and vitality it once did. If we see our lives full of problems versus challenges and opportunities, we have let the difficult events in life beat us.

When life events occur, we perceive them through one or more of our five senses: sight, hearing, taste, smell, and touch. Maybe one reason a walk in a forest seems to bring us "alive" is that it excites all of our senses and awakens us all at once. Nature lovers point to the healthful and healing effects of exposing our senses to the elements of the outdoors, like simply walking barefoot in the grass. We might not even notice some aspects of nature, such as the smell of fresh air during a thunderstorm. Our senses are channels for health as well as for information about our world.

Some say that as human beings we also have a sixth sense, like intuition, or a psychic sense, that lies dormant in some and is active in others. We come to know the world around us through those conscious or unconscious senses.

We learn about life through direct experiences and later through the stories of others—their beliefs, values, principles, and general wisdom. All our senses are working full-time from the moment of birth, perhaps even before birth, to help us create our mindsets about the world we live in. Who are the people and the situations we can trust and who are the people and situations that might cause us harm?

Internal Maps of Reality

In his powerful self-help book on meditation and finding inner peace, *Thresholds of the Mind*, Bill Harris likened our mindsets to "internal maps of reality."[12] Like a map used to navigate a city, a mental map is not the actual territory but a representation of the territory that allows us to navigate our way. A mental map is not reality but a representation of reality. And like any map, a mental map doesn't always exactly represent reality. As the territory or the reality around us changes, a map must be updated to guide us in the right direction.

Instead of creating limiting thinking from difficult life experiences, the emotionally healthy thing to do is to "let go" of those mindsets and replace them with attitudes that will lead us toward the lives we want to lead.

We hold onto some thinking because of the strength of our previous learning experiences, when in fact the territory around us, the reality of life's events, has changed. We cling to difficult life experiences, hoping that somehow we can avoid any more pain in the future. In reality, we are simply locking ourselves into a way of thinking and behaving in a way that will not help us get what we really want.

The keys are how we choose to frame those events—the stories we tell ourselves—and our habits in framing the world around us. Framing is taking the pool of raw data we perceive through our senses and adding meaning or an interpretation to create a story around it. For example, do you like the majority of the songs on today's top forty commercial radio stations? Based on when you were born, those songs can hold widely different interpretations and meanings.

The Paths of Choice model is the Choice Cycle in operation and taken to the next level of detail—a magnification of the choices we make every moment. It's really about the fundamental habits we have in seeing life events either as problems that confound us or as challenges to be overcome.[13]

A Challenge or a Problem?

Seeing difficult life events as challenges rather than problems is really an issue of "emotional intelligence," a phrase coined by Daniel Goleman in his book of the same name. As Goleman's research asserts, only about twenty percent of success in life is due to IQ, or intelligence quotient, the indicator we most often use to describe relative intellectual capacity. Eighty percent of success is due to other factors, such as our EQ, or emotional intelligence. Emotional intelligence includes abilities like "being able to motivate oneself and persist in the face of frustrations; to control impulse and delay gratification; to regulate one's moods and keep distress from swamping the ability to think; to empathize and to hope."[14]

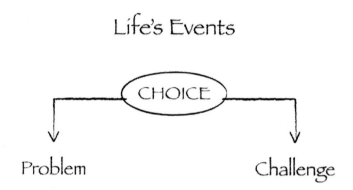

Have you ever thought about the difference between a challenge and a problem? Every year, many people climb Mount Everest, an adventure with incredible difficulties, including extreme cold, lack of oxygen, lack of food, and the ever-present possibility of life-threatening storms. Every trip runs the risk of sudden, unexpected death.

Sports Illustrated reports there is one death for every eight and a half people who reach the summit![15] Jon Krakauer did an amazing job of capturing the intensity of a Mount Everest climb in his book, *Into Thin Air*. And yet since New Zealand's Sir Edmund Hillary and Sherpa Tenzing Norgay first officially accomplished the feat in 1953, Everest has hosted close to two thousand successful climbs to the summit.

We regularly choose to face life-threatening dangers for the chance to overcome obstacles and succeed. Why? George Mallory, the British climber who made the first known serious attempt to climb Everest in 1921, possibly was right when he asserted, "Because it's there." Maybe, however, there is *more* to the story.

One way to think about a challenge versus a problem is that a problem is a difficult situation we would like to avoid, while a challenge is a difficult situation that we *choose* to engage in.

Could we consciously decide to choose our problems and think of them as challenges?

If difficult challenges are inevitable in life, why do we always want to avoid them, instead of learning what we are made of by taking them on as opportunities? Difficult life challenges will surface. Could we make a conscious choice to experience them without dread or annoyance and think of those events simply as obstacles from which we learn?

If we decide to commit to a mission of personal growth and learning in life, what is the purpose of an obstacle? One view is that an obstacle provides the means by which we can learn and grow. If our purpose is to learn as many lessons as we can, then life provides us with a wonderful abundance of opportunities!

If one of the primary reasons we are on this earth is to learn life's lessons—to learn and grow—shouldn't we welcome whatever life provides us?

Would we want to live a life with very few challenges? Probably not! Could we? Probably not! The real difference is not in the life events but how we view them. What we resist persists. Trying to escape problems reduces our chances of finding constructive solutions. Problems tend to stay until we find ways to address them.

Another way to look at it is that a challenge is a problem for which we already have a learning set; that is, we understand some basic principles that will ultimately help us resolve it. A computer problem to an IT specialist is a challenge, for instance, but to a neophyte user it can become a crisis.

Our ability to learn new concepts is a fundamental learning set that we can carry into any situation. Other examples of learning sets are the ability to remain emotionally calm, a willingness to try new behaviors, and a capacity to remain alert and learn from the results we get.

Believe in Yourself

A few years ago I spoke to representatives of Domino's Pizza in Ann Arbor, Michigan, about conducting an adventure-learning program for some of their managers. We talked about doing a high ropes course, which is a specialized series of physical events that require participants to climb and navigate structures that range from five feet to fifty feet above the ground. In the process, they learn a lot about their inner courage, improve their teamwork skills, and find ways to build trust with others. Many who first learn about a ropes course ask, "Why in the world would I want to do *that*?" Almost all who have actually done a ropes course know that it can be a very powerful, life-shaping experience.

The ropes course session was intended to serve as a reward for several high-performing teams that Domino's called "Beast Teams." A Beast Team was a group of hand-selected, high-performing managers who descended on the very lowest performing stores in the franchise and worked there for six months with a goal of using best practices to turn that store around. Six months later the Beast Team would move to another bottom performer and do it all over again, a never-ending cycle. Domino's Beast

Teams had had a very successful year, and they deserved a special reward for their efforts.

Tom Monaghan was the chairman and CEO of Domino's Pizza, the successful restaurant chain he had founded with his brother, James, in 1960. Tom not only wanted to do a high ropes course, he wanted to do the outdoor session in the middle of January in Michigan, *and* he wanted to require participants to camp out on the ropes course overnight.

This begs the question: If a January ropes course in Michigan including an overnight campout was considered a reward, what might Domino's do to the Beast Teams who underperformed? It took me a while to understand the value proposition in this idea, but Tom Monaghan had a plan.

He spent some formative years in the U.S. Marines, and he knew the benefits of surviving a rigorous training exercise. After his father died when Tom was only four years old, Tom's mother, Anna, had trouble raising him and his brother by herself. She sent them to an orphanage, St. Joseph Home for Children, in Jackson, Michigan. Tom and James also lived in a series of foster homes. One can only imagine the difficulties they experienced at such young ages, especially the feelings of abandonment and loss. Tom Monaghan was an unlikely candidate to start a highly successful, worldwide franchise.

Tom joined the U.S. Marine Corps in 1956, and the experience gave him confidence and courage. He gained self-efficacy—a belief that he could make something of himself—and he turned that inner strength into a successful business worth millions of dollars.

The gift that Tom Monaghan wanted to give his Beast Team managers was the insight to believe in themselves and the assurance that they could do anything they set their minds to. Like other participants on a high ropes course, they would realize that, with the support of each other, they could accomplish amazing things—even though they would have doubts when they started.

They would find the right clothes to wear and build a fire to stay warm. They would buy the right tents and sleeping bags, and they would find a way to have fun in the process. And when the sun rose the next morning, they would be alive and they would have accomplished an amazing feat. It was something the average person would never do.

What are the limitations of human beings? Tom Monaghan had learned through first-hand experience. There really are few limitations.

How does someone come to know that the biggest limitations are inside of us and not in the world around us? By starting to view difficult obstacles as challenges to be solved, not problems to be avoided. That's the core of it—how we think about the world around us and the challenges we face.

Usually, when we perceive an event as a problem, we say something like, "Oh no!" What we are thinking is, "Oh no, here we go again!" or, "Oh no, things are going to be really screwed up now!" We imagine that we are losing control of everything we have worked to build and that life is headed straight down into a death spiral.

In a nanosecond, we begin to experience at least some level of fear—fear of losing something, like control of the world around us. Fear is one of the strongest "learning disabilities," and as soon as it grips us, we lose the ability to act rationally and to learn from our results.

The physiological response to fear is stress, and we quickly begin to experience the symptoms of a stress reaction. In human beings that reaction includes a rush of adrenalin to give us strength to fight or to flee. Our hearts beat faster to send oxygen to our muscles; the pupils of our eyes expand in size so we can more readily detect the danger at hand, and our muscles tense. These are genetic responses that we have naturally sustained as survival techniques. We have survived because of our ability to respond appropriately to physical dangers.

Dangers we perceive in today's world are more often psychological not physical. Those responses can be damaging to our health, especially when we remain in fear and stress modes for long periods of time.

When we are under stress, there are two classic responses: We tend to either *fight*, attacking the perceived danger or person responsible for it, or *flee*, escaping or somehow getting away from the threat. Unfortunately, when we are fighting or fleeing, we are not responding in ways that get us the results we want. We become frozen in our emotional reactions and our responses are limited in their complexity and in their effectiveness.

How long does it take us to get from a life event to a non-resourceful response at the bottom of this response chain? In the blink of an eye!

Fight or Flee? Or Learn?

A negative emotional reaction to a perceived problem inhibits our ability to learn new things. A portion of the brain that helps us process emotional reactions is called the amygdala. It may serve as the source of an emotional response before we fully understand what is happening. The amygdala takes on the job of signaling our emotional centers to react. The cerebral cortex, or "thinking" part of our brains, is triggered next. If we can stay calm and see obstacles as simply challenges, we enhance our ability to have resourceful responses and increase our chances of successfully in dealing with situations.

An alternative is to consciously choose to see the world around us—even when it behaves far from our expectations—in a different way. This doesn't mean looking at the world with rose-colored glasses. We can't just agree to use the word *challenge* in lieu of the word *problem* and think that all of our pain and suffering will go away. I am suggesting a fundamental shift in the way we see and even feel about the world around us: to see *challenges* instead of *problems*.

A first step is to *focus*, to ask ourselves the questions, "What do I want?" or "What are the results I want to get?" and "What do I need to do to get what I want?"

The next step is to try something—to take some action toward creating the desired results. Take some time for reflection, but don't get stuck. Take some kind of action. Do something.

By focusing on what we want and taking some action, we may learn something from the results we get and be able to respond in a more effective way the next time. We may get fired, but if we do, we will find another job. Worst of all, we may make a mistake and look foolish! If we do, we can gather up the pieces, learn from our actions, refocus, and try again. This is when the most effective learning occurs.

The point here is to get into a *learning loop* instead of a fighting or fleeing loop. The outcome is much different. Even though we will not always be successful, in the end, we will have a much better chance at responding to situations effectively.

Life's Events

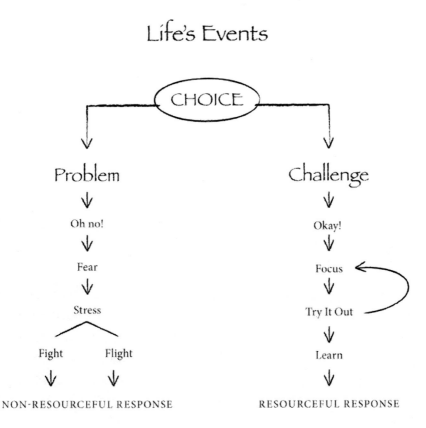

Another way to view these two paths is that the one to the left, seeing life events as problems, is the path of *playing not to lose.* What is playing not to lose? It's playing it safe, being risk-averse, laying low, not innovating, and doing the minimum required.

The path on the right, seeing a world of challenges, is the *playing to win* path. Playing to win is a willingness to take risks, to try new things, to innovate, to look foolish and sometimes be wrong, but to take action.

A Victim or a Survivor?

Another way to consider these fundamentally different paths is by choosing to be a "victim" or to be a "survivor." I don't mean to discount the notion of a true victim of very difficult life events that we don't control, such as being a victim of child abuse, a violent crime, or a drunk driver. What I'm describing is having a "victim mindset," or the tendency to look outside of ourselves to find someone or something to blame for events that we don't like. We think like victims at times. We look for ways to assign responsibility to some factor outside of ourselves. Humans are masters at finding reasons to stop trying. Holding onto a victim mindset and blaming others is the opposite of being personally accountable.

The survivor path, on the other hand, is the route we take when we assume personal accountability for the results we get, and we are willing to learn in the process. Surviving is about finding ways to improve not only our personal accountability but our response-ability—the ability to choose increasingly more effective stories, emotions, and behaviors, which then create the results we want.

Pause-Reflect-Act

As fallible human beings, however, it's important to remember there is no permanent transformation, and even with lots of practice we are going to migrate to the path of the victim from time to time. One key point of the Paths of Choice model is that we need to catch ourselves when we are on the victim path and move over to become survivors. How do we do that? I suggest a tool called "pause, reflect, and act."

- <u>Pause</u>: First, observe what you are doing and what you are getting back. Stop for a moment and simply see what is going on. Breathe deeply and think clearly. Lots of oxygen to the brain can work wonders.

- <u>Reflect:</u> Second, notice how you are looking at the current situation. Challenge the stories you are telling yourself about the pool of data. Are the stories real or imagined? Reflect upon the reasons why you are choosing to upset yourself. Challenge yourself by asking the question, "What do I really want here?"

- <u>Act</u>: Finally, choose the story, the emotion, and the behaviors that will get you the results that you want to achieve, and take action. Go for it!

Life's Events

What are some of the conclusions we are led to with the Paths of Choice model?

1. We influence the outcomes we get by the way we think and feel about what happens around us.

2. We have a vital role to play in our success; that is, we are personally accountable for the results that we create, whether we accept that philosophy or not.

3. We choose our reactions to life's events, and the choices we make can have a lot to do with the outcomes.

4. If I want different results, "**I**" have to do something different, not wait for the world around me to change. Who is responsible for the results that I get? "**I am!**"

Anything Is Possible

There's no future in believing something can't be done. Quotes from famous persons in our past demonstrate how, as human beings, we often limit our thinking about what is possible. Here are a few of my favorites:

...

"Everything that can be invented has been invented."
- Charles H. Duell, Director of U.S. Patent Office, 1899, in testimony to
Congress about why the U.S. Patent Office should be eliminated.

"Who the hell wants to hear actors talk?"
- Harry M. Warner, Warner Brothers Pictures, 1927.

"Sensible and responsible women do not want to vote."
- Grover Cleveland, U.S. President, 1905.

"There is no likelihood that man can ever
tap the power of the atom."
- Robert Millikan, Nobel Prize in Physics, 1923.

"Heavier than air flying machines are impossible."
- Lord Kelvin, President, Royal Society, 1895.

"Ruth made a big mistake when he gave up pitching."
- Tris Speaker, professional baseball player, 1921,
talking about Babe Ruth.

"There is no reason for any individual to
have a computer in their home."
- Kenneth Olsen, president and founder of
Digital Equipment Corporation, 1977.

"Computers in the future may ...
perhaps only weigh 1.5 tons."
- Popular Mechanics, forecasting the development
of computer technology, 1949.

"This 'telephone' has too many shortcomings to be seriously
considered as a means of communication."
- Western Union internal memo, 1876.

"I think there is a world market for about
five computers."
- Thomas Watson, chairman of the board, IBM, 1943.

...

What conclusion can we draw from these quotes? First, don't ever let someone write down what you say! People could be laughing at you someday!

Seriously, these are quotes from very intelligent individuals. They were using the best information they had at the time, based on commonly-held stories. Some insights into determining what truth is:

- A commonly-held mindset doesn't make it the truth.
- Very intelligent people—all of us, in fact—hold mindsets that inhibit our effectiveness. What do you think people will say about us one hundred years from now? Five hundred years from now? We are holding ourselves back in ways we don't even see yet.
- There are *always* opportunities to be more effective and to get better outcomes.

I would like to share with you some of my assumptions about what is possible.

First, I choose to believe that anything is possible. I am not sure if this is true, but I know that if I choose to believe anything is possible, I will constrain my thinking less. I am the only person who can change my mindsets. We might as well assume that anything is possible, because we really don't know what is possible, and as soon as we assume something is impossible, someone else will come along and prove us wrong.

Second, we have learned twelve percent of what is possible. That number isn't born of rigorous research—I made it up. But I think it is close enough. The point is we are not anywhere close to being knowledgeable about the universe outside of us or even inside of us. We have a lot to learn. We think of ourselves as an advanced society, but five hundred years from now people will laugh at our ignorance.

Third, we protect our egos with stories. Our egos tell us that we are okay, that we know enough already, and don't need to change what we know. Our egos keep us from learning new things that are contrary to what we think we already know.

Finally, learning occurs when we let go of what we already know. We have to let go of old mindsets and old stories to accept new ones that will get us better results. We are the ones who need to change, not the world around us. Correction: **I am the one who needs to change!**

CHAPTER 5

MIND, BODY, AND SPIRIT

"When we talk about settling the world's problems,
we're barking up the wrong tree.
The world is perfect. It's a mess. It has always been a mess.
We are not going to change it.
Our job is to straighten out our own lives."

—Joseph Campbell

The very first step in finding personal balance in our lives is to accept personal accountability for our balance.

We are living in a time when we are bombarded with messages that say "it is not your problem!" Attorneys encourage us to get our just dues. Newspapers sell copy by opening our eyes to the faults of the institutions around us. Television and movies tell a good story by finding villains in government, big business, and sometimes in the church.

There are definitely villains out there, but the residual of the media's message is that we are constantly looking for them.

Management races to get offshore in search of low-cost labor, sometimes viewing their employees as the core problem. Organized labor finds the blame in poor management decisions and actions. Each knows they are working hard and doing their part to make things better, so it must be someone else who is to blame!

In the West, we have become a culture of victims looking for *someone* to blame. And when it comes to finding personal balance in our lives, our first tendency is to look outside of ourselves, when the first step instead is to remember that *"I am responsible for the outcomes in my life."*

If we wait for our organizations and institutions to solve the challenge of personal balance for us, we will die unhappy, unbalanced people. Let's start by looking inside first. When we do, we observe a complex human mosaic of interconnected factors relating to finding balance and holistic health. As human beings, we are all affected by health in mind, in body, and in spirit.

True Self

As we navigate through this complex world we create façades, or *personal brand images*, to communicate to the world around us who we would like others to believe we are. We learn the façades that say "I am smart," "I am successful," "I am right," or "I am in control." These messages are born from our egos and are attempts to let others know that we are okay the way we are. We don't really need to change. Life is working just fine.

Unfortunately, after a lifetime of presenting this pretense to the world around us, we begin to believe in our own marketing. Instead of showing others our vulnerabilities, we begin to actually believe we are in control of it all, and we don't really need the support of others. "I can do it alone, thanks!"

Some use the expression "true self" to describe the person inside, at our core. Finding our true self is about rediscovering the part of ourselves that has always existed inside and is still there after we strip the shells we've built to protect ourselves in a fearful world. It is about finding that peaceful person and that serene place inside.

Our true self is the part of us that is always in balance, no matter what is going on around us. Finding personal balance is about doing the *inner work* to choose peace, no matter what the situation. Whenever we are ready, the great news is that our true selves are there waiting to be rediscovered.

Personal balance can be about work-life balance, about work-fun balance, or simply about being healthy. But at a deeper level, the goal of personal balance is ultimately about finding some peace of mind and joy in life, no matter what the circumstances. Like our true selves, personal balance is always there for us to rediscover. As we search for health in mind, body, and spirit, we don't need anything except the willingness to look inside to find it and to do the things most of us already know how to do.

The Fetzer Institute

"The key to humanity's future lies in the productive linkage of the mind, body, and spirit."

—John Fetzer

John Earl Fetzer was born in 1901 and was just sixteen when he built his first radio transmitter-receiver. In 1923, at age twenty-two, Fetzer built his first radio station for Emmanuel College (later known as Andrews University), eventually becoming a media pioneer of radio, television, cable, and even closed-circuit music systems. Through the power of his business empire, John

Fetzer earned enough money to buy the Detroit Tigers, who under his ownership won the World Series in 1968.

Fetzer later founded Fetzer Cablevision and upon his death in 1991, most of his wealth was endowed to the John E. Fetzer Foundation, which is called the Fetzer Institute today. The Fetzer Institute's mission focuses on the power of love and forgiveness to transform individuals and communities. A good deal of its early focus was to complement the traditional medical model with alternative research. The Institute's triangular logo symbolizes the connection between the three elements of wholeness embodied in mind, body, and spirit. A good deal of the Fetzer Institute's focus has been away from a traditional medical model and concentrated on alternative research.

This unique interest all started with Fetzer himself, who had a lifelong interest in "unseen forces," which included radio waves, but also parapsychology and spirituality. Within a 1900s culture that was indoctrinated with the philosophy of scientific method, Fetzer was unique in attending to the mental and spiritual forces at work in our total health. Instead of focusing exclusively on physical health, he realized the potential in understanding the *whole* person.

The ingredients of holistic health that interested John Fetzer have been expressed in different ways throughout history, and it is apparent that if we want balance in our lives, we need to consider the whole person. Inspired by John Fetzer's legacy, the framework of a personal balance plan contains five building blocks:

1. *Mind*: What is the impact of our mindsets? How do we think about the world around us, and how do we harness perhaps the strongest untapped resource in existence, the human mind?

2. *Body*: How can we take care of our physiological health and build upon the connection between our physical underpinnings and our emotional health?

3. *Spirit*: What are the connections between spiritual growth and peace in our lives? How can we employ some form of meditative practice to still the waters, to bring a sense of calm to our lives? How do we become a part of something bigger than ourselves?

4. *Changing the Game*: How can we define our priorities and reduce the complexity in our lives? How can we create structural solutions to the health of our minds, our bodies, and our spirits?

5. *Support*: How can we create the right support system in our lives—one that will help us be who we really want to be?

In the following chapters I explore each of these elements, one at a time, and allow space for you to reflect on each segment of your own personal plan. You know best what will work for you.

CHAPTER 6

FREE THE MIND

"Change your thoughts, and you change your world."

—Norman Vincent Peale

A Zen Parable

A Zen master was walking along slowly in the forest, deep in solemn meditation, when suddenly he noticed a large tiger coming his way. The Zen master started to run away but came to the edge of a cliff, with no place to go.

The holy man noticed a thick vine that ran down the side of the cliff, grabbed hold of it, and started his descent to the bottom, leaving the tiger behind. As he approached the bottom and apparent safety, he suddenly noticed another large tiger at the base of the cliff. He quickly scampered back up the vine, with one tiger lurking at the top of the cliff and the other pacing at the bottom.

The Zen master found a narrow ledge to perch upon while he considered his next steps. At least he had found a place to rest for a moment, so he would have time to think. As he was contemplating his choices, the Zen master noticed a small mouse gnawing on the vine above him. As the vine began to splinter, he began to imagine a dire ending.

Just then, the Zen master looked to his right and noticed a strawberry plant growing in a crevice, just within arm's length. The plant sported a single large, juicy, luscious strawberry.

So the Zen master took the action he knew he must: He ate the strawberry!

Some of us Western thinkers wouldn't have come to this conclusion. Many of us would try to solve the holy man's problem by feeding the strawberry to the mouse or by using it to distract the tigers in some way. A good Zen story has an underlying message, however, that looks at the metaphorical first, then the practical.

In this oft-told tale, the tigers represent the demons that keep us from enjoying a fulfilling life. The tiger at the top of the cliff, where we have been, represents the demons from our past, like anger, resentment, frustration, blame, guilt, or sorrow. The tiger at the bottom of the cliff, where we are going, represents fear or worry about the future. The real demons *we* face, of course, are those inside of us—the demons that keep us from finding balance, peace, and joy in our lives.

The fundamental lesson of this Zen parable is about freeing our minds to let go of whatever thinking holds us in a negative place. Freeing the mind is about examining the mindsets at play when we experience a negative emotion and learning how to let go of those mindsets so we either accept our circumstances or find the power within us to change them. We don't always have a choice about the challenging events in our lives, but we do have a choice about how we respond to them.

The story of Viktor Frankl in Chapter 2 reminds us that we have the last freedom, that is, the freedom to choose our attitudes and feelings, no matter the situation.

We easily slip into playing the victim or assuming others are the villains, the bad guys causing our grief. In reality *we* are the only ones who can create our stress or, conversely, let it go.

Freeing the mind is about letting go—releasing whatever meaning we attach to the events in our lives that cause us pain and suffering and replacing it with assumptions, mindsets, and self-talk that create a more positive mindset.

. . .

"Any fact facing us is not as important
as our attitude towards it,
for that determines our success or failure."
~ Norman Vincent Peale

. . .

We create stories about the world around us. We "frame" it, and in a way, we create our stress. The events don't create stress; we create our own stress through the meaning that we pile on top of the difficult events in our lives.

If we only understand twelve percent of what is really going on in the universe, we don't know enough to be pessimists!

The Four Noble Truths

Followers of Buddhism claim "Four Noble Truths." These were first shared by Buddha at the Deer Park at Sarnath in 528 BC, and have been kept alive by Buddhist literature and lore ever since. The first two Noble Truths are lessons about freeing the mind:

1. *Life has suffering.* Sometimes written as "life is suffering," this message was reworded as the opening sentence in Scott Peck's *The Road Less Traveled*: "Life is difficult." Challenges are a part of this package we call life, so don't assume otherwise. Whoever coined the phrase "life is a beach" must have been trying to convey that sometimes the winds of life blow sand in our eyes! We need to accept that and get used to it.

   Those who commit their lives to personal growth understand that the reason for suffering, and maybe for our entire flesh and blood existence, is that challenges bring with them lessons about life, assuming we respond in a healthy way. If we don't, the lessons can be lost. But let's just get used to the fact that life for all of us is difficult, no matter how fortunate another's life appears from a distance.

   Let's get rid of this notion that if we do all of the right things in life, we can avoid challenges. Let's accept a reality that says if I solve all of my problems, there are more waiting in line. There is no guarantee of permanent health, wealth, and happiness, even if we continue to look for silver bullet solutions. (*"All you have to do is order by midnight tonight!"*) We often don't have a choice in what life brings us, only in how we respond to it.

2. *The source of all suffering is desire.* The lesson here is to detach oneself or to let go of whatever we are holding onto that keeps the suffering in place. An inherent life lesson is embedded in letting go of whatever keeps us in place. This is especially true when we think about the world

around us, and changing our non-resourceful mindsets is at the heart of it.

Can you let go of whatever desire is causing your suffering? That is the key to growth and also the key to finding personal balance.

We get ego-stroking benefits from holding onto our thinking, especially believing we are powerless victims in a world out of our control. If we allow ourselves to accept personal accountability, the hard work to make a difference falls squarely in our laps. It's a lot easier to find blame somewhere else, like the organization that forces us to do too much stressful work.

Each of us tends to hold onto desires that define our comfort zones. We acquire emotional *specialties* that persist as themes in our lives or as fears that we do not want to let go of. Some examples:

- I want or need to be in control.
- I want or need to win or at least to never lose.
- I want or need to be recognized by others for my accomplishments.
- I want or need to get attention from others.
- I want or need to have status in a group.
- I want or need to be served by others.
- I want or need to get approval from others.
- I want or need to be loved by everyone.
- I want or need to be right and avoid mistakes or at least avoid being wrong.

- I want or need to save face and not be embarrassed.

- I want or need to remain emotionally comfortable.

- I want or need to always be satisfied, and quickly!

Does one or more of these fit you? Do you know of others that are not on the list? When not satisfied, these deep desires we hold continue to cause us suffering.

Bill Harris, founder of the Centerpointe Research Institute, espouses nine principles for conscious living. His first is "Let whatever happens be okay."

Harris' point is that all of our suffering results from our *resistance* to reality, rather than first accepting *what is*. No matter what is going on in our lives, a first step is accepting that everything is perfect and whatever happens should happen. Next, we can decide to change what is to an outcome that we would prefer, or we can choose to accept the current situation. Emotional resistance to the current state adds frustration on top of the job of taking action to create new outcomes.

···

The Serenity Prayer:
"God, grant me the serenity to accept
the things I cannot change,
the courage to change the things I can,
and the wisdom to know the difference."
- Reinhold Neibuhr

···

Letting whatever happens be okay is a mental shift, a change in a fundamental mindset that our role is to judge the world around us, to decide what is good and what is bad. One who chooses a role of judgment is committing to a life of frustration, anger, and disillusionment.

The point here is not apathy, to just accept anything that happens. The lesson is in understanding and then simply preferring different outcomes, not holding our happiness hostage until we get them. When possible, we should take steps to get better results, but being upset usually doesn't help.

The challenge for each of us is to examine our own lives and to discover the desires and needs we cling to that become the sources of our suffering. Another way to get a peek into our mindsets is to listen to our "self-talk." Our self-talk is what we say to ourselves, usually covertly, when we experience any life event. When attempting to quit smoking, one might say, "I really want a cigarette, but I am going to fight it as long as I can!" Or, the self-talk might be simply, "I will *never* smoke another cigarette!"

This first example of self-talk is an expression of a mindset or a story that represents powerlessness or heroic effort but lack of real choice in the face of addiction. The second example is an affirmation based on a belief that we always have the choice in our behavior and the final freedom to decide, no matter what. Someone who is *trying* to quit smoking probably won't. Someone who really *decides* to quit smoking has a better chance at success. Self-talk is so important to success in the face of any difficult challenge.

...

"Our heads are round
so our thinking
can change direction."
- Francis Picabia

...

What we say to ourselves is an outcome of what we believe about the world around us. What we believe is critical, especially in difficult life challenges like finding personal balance.

Henry Ford was quoted as saying, "Believe you can or believe you can't. Either way you are right." I think he nailed it.

There are innumerable ways to reflect on the effects of thinking on our behavior, but fundamentally, it is all about one's intention and choice. The most powerful resource we can have in accomplishing a difficult challenge is the human mind. Set it free to work for you.

Application and Notes

Take a moment to think of your own difficult life challenges, emotional pain, or stress, and write your answers:

1. What is a story (a mindset, mental map, attitude, assumption, or belief) that you could let go of?

2. What are some life challenges that you could frame in a different way?

Notes:

CHAPTER 7

PREPARE THE BODY

"We don't see things as they are; we see them as we are."

—Anais Nin

Finding personal balance is about doing the things we already know how to do to become the people that we already are. Taking care of our bodies is a critical element in our overall health and, in general, one most of us already know how to do. There is an abundance of educational programs and media dedicated to teaching the lessons of good health—what we put into and what we do with our bodies.

Lessons about preparing our bodies come back to *intention* and *choice*. Genetic factors are at play, such as in inherited tendencies for heart disease, cholesterol, and obesity, and yet that is the "hand that life deals us." Our health is largely based on how we play out that hand.

Good physical health, or simply feeling good physically, is vital in finding balance in a stressful world. Mountains go back to being molehills—crises come back into perspective—when we feel healthy.

The purpose of this chapter is not to cajole, to admonish, or to judge anyone, but simply to remind us that we have a choice. Doing one or two things to live healthier, maybe simply going to bed earlier to get a little more sleep, make a difference. Making *some* progress, even though slight, can add to a sense that things are getting better. That alone can make a difference.

Physical health may not be an absolutely essential element in the personal balance formula, but it helps.

Ray

On July 16, 2002, shortly after his forty-ninth birthday, my brother Ray tripped over something lying on the floor in his home. An ordinary, minor accident at home—something that happens every day and that could happen to any of us. For Ray, the consequences were much more severe. His head hit the corner junction of two walls. The impact caused a severe spinal cord injury, resulting in full paralysis below his neck. In a cruel instant of fate, laden with the suffering that life can bring, Ray had become a quadriplegic.

The horror of what had happened didn't really settle in at first. He lay on his floor for three hours before a friend found him, all the while thinking about the simple little trick that life had played on him, so mundane it couldn't possibly be that serious. Surely he would snap out of a short-term paralysis. Maybe, like many of the Sunday football players he had watched, Ray had just experienced a "stinger," a short-term injury to the nerves of his neck that would pass quickly.

But Ray's use of his arms and his legs didn't come back, ever. No matter how much he wanted them to, no matter how much he denied the results of a single, momentary act, no matter how many days he woke up in disbelief, ready to get back to normal life, Ray's life was changed. He went through all the stages of grief that Elisabeth Kübler-Ross taught us—denial, anger and blame, negotiation, depression, and then back through the cycle again and again, until he finally came to acceptance.

During some of my long bedside visits with Ray in the hospital, our conversations would wander everywhere. We talked about our past as young brothers growing up on a small farm in Michigan. Without video games or a lot of TV, we created our own sense of adventure in the woods, at the creek catching frogs, exploring together in Pine Gully, and sledding down Wessy's Hill.

We talked about the hard work on the farm that we were so anxious to move away from, but that upon reflection taught us so much about life to come. Life seemed so much simpler then. I guess it was.

We talked about how our lives can change in the blink of an eye, and how they never really turn out the way we plan.

And I will never forget one conversation we had.

"I am the happiest that I have ever been in my life," Ray told me.

Somehow, under the worst circumstances imaginable, his body in the worst physical health of his life, Ray had discovered firsthand Viktor Frankl's concept of the *last freedom*: to choose our attitude, our mindset, how we feel, and what we think, no matter what our circumstances.

Other heroic people have discovered and reported this same life lesson. They have been in prisoner of war camps, suffered paralysis, Lou Gehrig's Disease (amyotrophic lateral sclerosis), multiple sclerosis, terminal cancer, or many other challenges that present themselves in our lives when we least expect them. We can find peace in our lives, no matter what.

The lesson I learned from my brother Ray is that no matter what the condition of one's physical existence, we can lean back on the power of the human mind, and we can still find peace and joy in our lives. We always have the last freedom.

After numerous physical complications from his quadriplegia, Ray finally let go of this life in November of 2002, four short months after his accident. But I know that as my family sat in vigil by his bedside listening to his last breath, he left this world a happy man.

Any of us could find ourselves in circumstances where our physical health is not good and still find personal balance in our lives. However, as long as we *do* have the ability to positively influence our health—to eat right, to exercise, and to sleep well—our physical health can have a positive impact on our overall health. Mind, body, and spirit—all play a role.

The Seven Practices

Dr. Nedra Belloc was a pioneer in discovering the factors responsible for good physical health. With her associate researcher, Dr. Lester Breslow, Dr. Belloc conducted a long-term study of the lives of nearly seven thousand people living in Alameda County, California. Their classic research was conducted while they worked in the Human Population Lab and was published in *Preventative Medicine*.[16]

Drs. Belloc and Breslow identified seven critical lifestyle factors that influence how long a person lives:

1. Maintain proper weight.

2. Moderate or no use of alcohol.

3. Sleep seven to eight hours nightly.

4. Eat breakfast regularly.
5. No eating between meals.
6. Regular physical exercise (twenty or more minutes, three days a week).
7. No smoking.

In 1973, living with six or seven of these habits for at least nine years earned men an additional eleven years of life expectancy and women an additional seven years. In 1970, the average life expectancy at birth was sixty-seven years for men and seventy-four years for women, so the increase was significant!

By 2004 in the United States, the average life expectancy for males was seventy-five years and just over eighty years for females. The seven health practices should certainly help one live even longer with today's better healthcare.

Recent advances in health practices suggest some slight modifications to the seven practices described by Dr. Belloc. Some research suggests that five or six small meals spread throughout the day are healthier than the three larger, traditional meals of breakfast, lunch, and dinner. Eating between meals may be less of an issue than originally thought.

I suppose a late night raid on the freezer to eat ice cream or scrounging in the pantry for potato chips would not qualify as one more small meal for the day! We humans have an infinite source of creativity when it comes to rationalizing our behavior, but we mostly know what good eating practices are for each of us, given our metabolism and how we feel afterward.

There is an abundance of new press around the health benefits of red wine (a rich source of antioxidants, including flavonoid phenolics) and even chocolate (helps the body process nitric oxide). Woohoo! Finally some good news from the pundits who have warned me for years that I am going to die from everything I like!

Well, maybe we shouldn't get *too* excited yet. Studies have shown that alcohol might increase triglycerides, and we know it can result in weight gain. Other research suggests a connection to cancer, especially colon cancer. Moderation in everything seems to come back over and over again as a good guiding principle. Balanced, of course, with the right level of fun and enjoyment in this life we live. Don't save everything for the end. Enjoy a little ice cream on the journey!

Physicians who attend my workshop on "Personal Balance Planning" do confirm what we already know, that the meals we eat are healthier when they include lots of fruits and vegetables and limited portions of red meat. Also, they remind me that staying hydrated by drinking sufficient amounts of water or other healthy liquids helps to keep our bodies healthy.

The physical exercise guideline of three times a week for a minimum of twenty minutes is another parameter that has come under challenge. Some say an hour a day, six days a week is the right amount. Twenty minutes a day for three days a week is better than no exercise at all, however, and any exercise is better than being a full-time couch potato. We need to get attuned to the messages that our bodies send us and do what we can.

And do what we can sustain. Working out vigorously for the first three days after a New Year's resolution will not be enough for the rest of the year. My suggestion is to do *something* and to find the people in your life who will support you in doing the things that are healthy for you. (More on support later, in Chapter 10.)

Fighting the Degenerative Diseases

We are living long enough today to die from degenerative diseases, including, in order: heart disease, cancer, stroke, chronic lower respiratory diseases, and diabetes. In 1900, cardiovascular disease was also listed as the leading cause of death, but the next two leading causes were influenza and pneumonia, followed closely by tuberculosis. In the U.S. and in other countries with abundant and effective healthcare, we have mostly controlled viral and bacterial disease. Today we are dying from the degeneration of our bodies.

There is promising news behind these statistics. Through good health practices, we may help ward off degenerative diseases. The real breakthrough from Nedra Belloc's and Lester Breslow's research was that inherited traits are not the primary factors in how we live or how we die. Their seven factors prove to us that we can take responsibility for many of the leading factors.

C. Everett Koop published the first *Surgeon General's Report on Nutrition and Health* in 1988 and reinforced the same point. Five of the ten leading causes of illness and death at the time (heart disease, cancer, stroke, diabetes, and atherosclerosis) were associated with diet.[17]

We have benefited from a wealth of scientific research into our health, and there aren't any big surprises here. Most of us know these factors, but many of us make daily choices that aren't in our best long-term interests.

More recent books on healthy diet and exercise practices have advanced our understanding of how our bodies work and how to stay healthy. In *The Best Life Diet*, fitness trainer Bob Greene advocates a three-phase plan and his own six rules in phase one:

- Eat three meals every day, plus one snack.
- Start eating breakfast.
- Increase activity level (depending on what activity you do now).
- Eliminate alcohol (may be added back later).
- Take a multivitamin, an omega-3 supplement and a calcium supplement if you are not getting enough from your diet.
- Stop eating at least two hours before going to bed.[18]

Notice the reassertion of the importance of breakfast, which Greene contends most Americans skip in their daily busyness. He also suggests a *gradual* approach, as in increasing one's activity level from the current state. Greene's approach seems workable because his emphasis is on starting where you are right now, not jumping dramatically to a plan that is not reasonable or sustainable.

Bob Greene's second phase is more challenging, with an emphasis on eliminating junk food from one's diet. Phase three leads to permanent lifestyle practices through changes implemented over time.

CNN's Chief Medical Correspondent, Dr. Sanjay Gupta, has also has written a book based on the latest available research that captures lessons from around the world. In *Chasing Life: New Discoveries in the Search for Immortality to Help You Age Less Today,* Dr. Gupta, a prominent neurosurgeon and medical journalist, describes stories of medical discoveries from around the world. He advocates eating well and eating less and not relying on nutritional supplements but finding vitamins and minerals in natural foods.[19]

Sanjay Gupta's message to us is about increasing our *health* span, not just our *life* span. The point is not just to live a long time, but to employ reported advances in science, diet, and exercise to improve the quality of our lives at advanced ages—to extend our *active lives*. He supports the notion that physical fitness can have a profound effect on cognitive ability, confirming a mind-body connection.

One of his messages is not directly related to diet or exercise, but centers on intention and focus. Having a sense of purpose in life is one of the factors that keeps us healthy, especially later in life. The classic stories of people passing away soon after retirement or after losing a loved one speak to the importance of having a clear focus in our lives, a reason to get out of bed in the morning. Again, the connection between our minds and our bodies is clear.

Do health practices that help us live longer also help us feel better? You bet. And that's really the point. Our overall psychological and emotional health is better when we feel better physically. They are undeniably linked.

When the state of our physical health is good, the events that come along in life that might cause us stress roll off our backs as nonevents. When we are feeling good, the world looks good around us. On the other hand, if we come to work with a hangover or without enough sleep, every little challenge can become a crisis.

An extreme case of this principle is evident with chronic drug and alcohol abuse. Addicts find themselves perpetually on or over the edge emotionally. Little problems become big issues and even affect a person's ability to perform simple daily tasks. Interactions with others can become constant screaming matches.

Is any of this behavior logical or rational? No, but it illustrates the power of the body over how we think and feel. After all, every thought and behavior has a physiological underpinning, and to take care of our balance, we need to start with the health of our bodies.

A reasonable approach may not include following all seven practices at once, but choosing just one thing to improve physical health. Some need a crisis to take that step, like when that heart attack we've always feared finally comes. A heart attack is a serious wake-up call from the body, telling us maybe it's time to start that exercise program we have been putting off forever.

And some create their own "crisis," a self-administered wake-up call, to get started. A personal jump start might be a week at a diet spa or perhaps hiring a personal coach at a health club. We usually know what to do. What we need is the will to get started.

Application and Notes

The key to improving physical health is to start somewhere. So start by answering these three questions:

1. What are you doing today to nurture your physical health?

2. What else *could* you do?

3. What else *will* you do?

Notes:

CHAPTER 8

RELEASE THE SPIRIT

"I know God promises not to give me more than I can handle.
I just wish He didn't trust me so much."

—Mother Teresa

The spiritual component of the mind-body-spirit connection is a sensitive discussion point because we all have differing world views and attitudes about the words *spiritual* and *spirit*. This is a very personal part of living a balanced life, and each of us needs to find our own path to spiritual fulfillment and growth.

I was fortunate to grow up in a large family with a strong religious and spiritual foundation. Every Sunday morning, my parents would somehow organize all eight of us kids, clean us up if our Saturday night baths had already been blemished, and get us all to church, pretty much on time. I have my dad to thank for his silent support and steely focus. With one quick glance, he could get all of us to jump in the car and sit quietly! But my mom deserves most of the credit for miraculously making it all happen every week.

Along with my family, the families from the surrounding farms who belonged to our Catholic church made the long trek into town each Sunday morning. Eventually, we convinced a "missionary" priest to drive out into the country to say mass for us. We began meeting every Sunday morning in various public buildings nestled in the southwestern Michigan countryside.

A couple of nearby dance halls worked well for the services. I was too young to know how we came by these facilities, but they served the purpose. I remember arriving early on some mornings to help clean up from the previous night's fun before the priest and the rest of the parishioners arrived.

Eventually the leaders of our small congregation raised the money and summoned the courage to build our own church. We relied on the generosity of one of our own to donate the land and somehow we scraped together the funds. We all, including the kids, pitched in and worked together with a spirit that must have been similar to a community barn raising.

My family took an active hand in Our Lady of Great Oak Church after it was built. My father was an usher, my mother worked in the altar society decorating the church, and my sister played the organ on Sundays. My two brothers and I served as the altar boys, taking turns and sometimes serving together. If this story sounds a little idealistic, well, I guess it is. To be honest, my participation was more an obligation than a great spiritual mission.

Something Bigger than Ourselves

Looking back on these early experiences with religion, like a great deal of my life, I was simply along for the ride. And yet, in the process, life's lessons emerged. While I didn't really do much work or serve out of any noble purpose, building that community church was the first time I had participated with a group of people who were on a mission and serving a purpose bigger than themselves. As an impressionable young man, the thirst for a mission—having some kind of special purpose—took hold.

Those who have been involved in an effort to do something important in life know that feeling. A "normal" life just isn't good enough any more. We become attached to the idea of making a difference in whatever small way we can and in need of becoming a part of something bigger than ourselves.

In order to find true fulfillment in our lives, *we need to become a part of something bigger than ourselves.*

At some point in our developmental cycles, whether we are religious or not, most human beings discover an open space inside that can only be filled by finding out what that "bigger something" is. We begin to explore our meaning and our relationship to the universe, to what Gandhi referred to as the "one source" of everything and everyone. Gandhi understood that inner peace comes from the one source in each of us, which in turn, ultimately unites all of us.

By whatever path one takes, those who have rich spiritual lives find an inner peace that gives them strength during difficult times. Spiritual strength may not be a prerequisite for joy in one's life, much as physical ailments can be neutralized by how we think. However, those who draw meaning from a deep spiritual source cannot imagine an existence without that dimension in their lives.

There is no denying we are spiritual beings in physical bodies and there is an inner spirit in each of us that is critically important to our overall health. Many of us find healing from the emotional pains in life though our spiritual connection. Having great spiritual strength alone can overcome any life challenge and create personal balance. Peace of mind and joy in life are available to those who are spiritually strong.

Today, someone who is interested in a revitalizing journey of spiritual growth has many options. Some contend there is one right path—theirs—but I am not wise enough to offer similar guidance. My hope is that we will learn to be more supportive of each other's spiritual journeys, along whatever paths they take. If one is not compelled by any formal religion, it is important to find a way that leads to inner peace.

There are many great religions in the world that have grown from the need for each of us to connect to our spiritual core. These religions have helped us find peace in our lives and peace in our losses. Every organized religion also suffers at times from the inherent politics involved in aligning large groups of people and from being guided by imperfect human beings.

Elements of a Spiritual Journey

While choosing a spiritual path is a very personal endeavor, my definition of spiritual doesn't depend upon selecting any dogma or religion. You might find your path to spiritual fulfillment in a religion or you might find it in some other way. The important thing is to have some sort of spiritual practice, a way to create spiritual growth in your life.

Three elements seem common to a rich spiritual practice:

1. *A Meditative Practice*: The first element of a spiritual journey is some form of regular meditative practice, prayer, or reflection—some activity that calms the waters for a time.

    One might experience this meditation in a church, in a synagogue, in a mosque, or in a quiet place at home. For some, a special place outdoors in nature may provide the perfect setting. Maybe it comes when you read an inspiring book, have a quiet talk with a close friend, or simply take a long walk.

Prayer is one example of a meditative practice, or one can pursue actual meditation and contemplation. One who is interested in true meditation can find guidance from a number of sources and schools of thought. The use of audio technology has been refined by Bill Harris at the Centerpointe Research Institute in creating his "Holosync" program. On its Web site, www.centerpointe.com, the Centerpointe Research Institute explains that alpha, theta, and even delta brain waves can be induced while guiding someone to deep states of relaxation and reflection, a process with proven results in thousands of people.

...

"In the midst of movement and chaos, keep stillness inside of you."
- Deepak Chopra

...

There are many personalized practices to adopt, including physical exercise and contemplative dialogue. The critical ingredient is reaching a state of deep relaxation and practicing being in a calm, personal space. It's important to find a way to go there on a regular basis.

2. *Focus On the Present Moment*: Focusing on the present moment while holding a core belief that in the end, no matter the challenge, everything will work out, is an important component of a spiritual path.

Some believe in an afterlife that offers hope for a better place and a reward for good living. Even if one doesn't accept an afterlife, focusing on the present moment is healthier than negative feelings about the past or worry about the future.

Some believe in reincarnation, which provides a broader perspective on a single life and also offers hope that, despite any challenges we face here in our physical form, a place of love and light follows.

Some believe in the Eightfold Path as laid out by Buddha, knowing that there is an end to suffering.

It is important to appreciate the moment, to believe that life will improve and that we are working toward something better. It is a mindset of *syntropy*, that life's ingredients are recombining into a higher order, and not *entropy*, that life is falling apart.

3. *Finding Meaning*: Meaning comes from being part of something bigger than oneself—a connection to a higher purpose in life—beyond simply surviving or "getting by."

For some this includes being connected to a religion or some system of faith. For others it might mean being of service to humankind, driven by a set of values that helps to leave the world a better place. Some might share an affinity with others to feed the hungry, to clothe the poor, or to provide shelter for those who are less fortunate.

Connection to others becomes a positive spiritual force when it is driven by a broader goal of making the world a better place. Commitment to increasing value to shareholders or protecting street gang turf can connect us, but neither seems to stimulate the same spiritual growth as volunteerism. A spiritual connection comes from being a part of a *greater good*, of doing something for the betterment of the world.

Your Spiritual Path

If you were asked to tell the story of your own spiritual growth and your spiritual practice, what would you say? Is it important to you? Have you started?

Perhaps spiritual growth has not been an important part of your life thus far, and maybe it never will. However, if you are searching for ways to find personal balance—inner peace and joy despite the craziness around us—the third leg of the mind-body-spirit stool can be an important one. As a tool in the constant battle to find some peace of mind, a healthy spiritual life can be all one really needs.

"It is pleasing to God whenever you rejoice or laugh
from the bottom of your heart."

—Martin Luther

Application and Notes
Write out some thoughts about your spiritual practice and what you might do to take another step in your spiritual growth:

1. What are the formative experiences in your spiritual journey?

2. What are some reflections about your spiritual practice today?

3. How do you nurture your spirit?

4. What is one new way to move your spiritual practice forward?

Notes:

CHAPTER 9

SIMPLICITY: CHANGING THE GAME OF LIFE

"May you live all the days of your life."

—Jonathan Swift

Dick Walls

A person who has made an incredible difference in my life is Dr. Richard T. Walls. One of my early mentors, Dick is a full professor at West Virginia University and one of the most productive individuals I have ever met. Dick has been publicly acknowledged by having his name carved into the "Honor Wall" in front of the WVU library twice, once for outstanding teaching and again as a distinguished scholar.

While a tenured professor with a full teaching load at the university, as well as a respected researcher and writer in vocational rehabilitation, Dick and his wife, Janet, decided to build their own house. Even though he was already a very busy man, Dick placed an old-fashioned importance on building his own home, like his West Virginia forefathers before him.

He could have easily survived as a pioneer two hundred years ago; he isn't afraid to try anything. In addition to his house, he has built a log cabin, rebuilt several vintage cars, assembled his own hot rod, constructed a second garage to store his cars, and even dug his own pond!

In West Virginia, neighbors and families still understand the value of helping each other in times of need. When he built his house, Dick got lots of help. However, he also knew about "sweat equity," and he achieved in every aspect of his life by taking action. In his office, Dick publicly posted a checklist, setting a goal to accomplish at least one task on his house every single day.

The job could have been helping the old Italian stone mason who used the rocks found on Dick's and Janet's property for the siding, or it might have been building a section of the stone retaining wall in the back yard. One day it might have meant helping Janet plant some of the scores of rhododendron bushes surrounding the house, and on another day it might have been sinking the deck posts. Just a little bit, every day.

Doing just one task seemed like a simple and a modest goal and not really that ambitious. It was a small amount that anyone could do, really. But his house was finished fast and the lesson for everyone who saw it happen was the cumulative power in doing just a little at a time. Suddenly, Dick and Janet had a new house.

Dick Walls did the same with his research publications, starting with a goal of one professional publication every year. Through steady discipline, he accomplished an even higher goal of three published research articles a year, each and every year. Today that collective effort has resulted in close to 140 published articles, books, and book chapters—an incredible body of work.

Dick used a disciplined technique in his writing that he called "punch a hole in it." At the end of the day, when I was tired and ready to pack it in, he would force me to sit with him to write just one paragraph on the next day's assignment.

"Oh come on, we can do it tomorrow!" was my regular protest, but Dick would say, "Come on—let's just punch a hole in it." And so we would write one more paragraph together for the day, maybe taking five to ten minutes.

Sure enough, when we started the next morning, the paragraph was already done, and we had a fast start to the day. Dick knew that a journey of a thousand miles begins with a single step, and often that first step can be the hardest. Take it, and the journey flows.

Setting goals as a way to focus on his priorities became a way of life for Dick. He has stayed on a regular daily exercise regime for nearly thirty years that has included Royal Canadian Air Force exercises, twenty minutes on the Nordic track, fifty sit-ups and fifty push-ups, weightlifting, and one hundred calf-raises. You can surely understand why I never asked Dick to become my personal trainer!

It was amazing to watch what could be accomplished with small goals and the discipline to execute them. Structuring our environments so that we keep our goals in front of our faces and do a little at a time is something we all know but few of us do. What is one small thing that we can do each day to define our priorities and to improve our personal balance?

Simplicity

Simplicity is all about changing the game by attending to the structural forces in our lives, including our goals, which affect our emotions and our behavior.

The design of our environments can have a big effect on us, from the obvious factors like physical safety risks and noise pollution to less obvious choices, such as the way we drive home. Taking the back roads for a more relaxing—albeit somewhat longer—drive home at the end of the day might vastly improve our mood when we walk in the front door.

Simplicity means we take control of the environmental factors that tend to elicit a response of stress or, alternatively, to encourage a response of inner peace. It is easy in a world where we are doing more with less to convince ourselves that we don't really have the time to reflect on our visions, to set goals, to take time for the most important things and not just the urgent things. Every day when we get up, the race is on!

We all know the story common to life in the fast lane. In an effort to save time, we don't sit down for breakfast, and we speed in our cars on our way to work, eyes darting side to side looking for radar traps. We move from meeting to meeting, slaves to our calendars, living lives that are driven by others. We stay at the office longer than most and we bring work home, hoping to catch up on some of the hundreds of e-mails we didn't touch during the day. We eat dinner in our home office or in front of the TV. When dinner doesn't completely quell our appetites and soothe our stress, we eat from our pantries, stocked with unhealthy late night snacks. We eat ice cream directly from the freezer, assuming that small bites don't really contain very many calories. We stay up too late because we are "wired," insisting on a little personal time at the end of the day (I deserve it!), only to start the cycle over again the next morning.

Each of these responses is a choice we make, conscious or otherwise, that affects our personal health. We're willing to sacrifice for the short term as we succumb to the illusion of impending stability, sure that our lives will slow down soon and then we can get back to normal. We're convinced that's what it takes to succeed in a competitive world.

We become attached to a certain pace of living and conveniently become victims of an ever-escalating speed of life and our own unhealthy choices. We medicate our stress and ourselves in many ways, often to the long-term disadvantage of our personal health.

Just as it takes a conscious decision to free the mind, it takes a conscious choice to simplify our lives. So what are the choices we could make that lead to a healthier, simpler life, especially for the limited time we have at home?

Changing the game—making healthier choices toward simplicity—means setting priorities. An easy rule for success that we know but we forget, is to set a goal (in this context, personal balance), then decide on the important ways to get there. We fill our lives with urgent tasks and forget our true priorities in life.

Practical Steps to Simplicity

A part of setting priorities is determining the activities to spend our time on, but it's also important to decide what we will *not* spend time doing. A "stop list" is just as important as a to-do list. What are we *not* going to do to create some reasonable pace or sense of focus in our lives? What would you be willing to walk away from to create more balance in your life?

Another way to change the game is to examine our eating habits. Are we taking time to slowly enjoy every bite of food, or unconsciously inhaling food we don't taste? Whenever possible, we could relax with family or friends, slowing the pace for a good conversation and some laughter when we eat. Social time and laughter help with digestion. Otherwise our meals become just another item to check off for the day. We get through them, but without the potential benefits of the relaxation and the social time.

One pattern to observe is how you start your day. Are you sleeping until the last moment and then racing to work in the fast lane, starting a habit that carries through the day? Alternatively, are you getting up a few minutes early to relax, to enjoy your morning routine, and to do some positive thinking on an enjoyable drive to work? A tone of rushing and being behind is hard to break away from if it starts when we roll out of bed.

Simplicity Ideas

Here are a few ideas for changing the game in your life. Some of these might work for you and some of them might not work, but you get the idea. *Your* list is the one that will work for you:

- Get up a few minutes early to allow for a relaxed pace in the morning.
- Schedule a regular physical exercise time.
- Schedule a regular meditation time.
- Have breakfast or just coffee or tea with someone you care about.
- Take a few minutes for prayer or reflection at the start of the day.
- Drive a slow way to work with a goal of relaxing on the way.

- Save your phone calls for the office, rather than use your cell phone along the way. Safe behavior reduces stress, too.
- Drive at or just under the speed limit to work.
- Eliminate or reduce loud and distracting noises in your environment.
- Play relaxing music on the drive to work and on the drive home. Play it at work if you can and it helps you. Music can create emotional moods, so use it to your advantage.
- Play a motivational CD, MP3, or radio station on the drive to work.
- Create a checklist of to-do items that you review at the beginning of the day. Ideally, create this list before you leave the day before *(punch a hole in it)*.
- Decide each day what you are *not* going to do. Have a stop list.
- Put low priority projects in a desk drawer to work on if you have extra time. Clean it out from time to time if nobody asks about them.
- Delete low priority e-mails.
- Share a code of behavior around e-mails with the people who send them to eliminate unnecessary correspondence.
- Create annual goals and objectives, and review your progress each month.
- Stop work that is not on your list of goals and objectives, or change your goals and objectives.
- Allow time to arrive at meetings on time.
- Block some time on your calendar when you will *not* attend meetings.
- Schedule time for dinner with family or friends.

- Consider the people who surround you. Do they encourage your growth or encourage you to be a victim? Spend time with people who support you in being who you want to be.
- Keep healthy food and snacks in your home, and keep unhealthy food out of your home and car.
- Others:

Application and Notes

Capture your thoughts on finding simplicity and changing the game in your life, and write down what you might do to take the next step:

1. What are your highest priorities, in order?

2. What do you want to spend the precious time in your life doing?

3. What could you walk away from or let go?

4. How could you change your physical environment or structure?

5. How else could you change the game you are playing to get different results?

Notes:

CHAPTER 10

CREATE SUPPORT

"We find ourselves by losing ourselves in the service to others."

—Mahatma Gandhi

Trisha Meili

From time to time, people come into our lives with special lessons for us. In my life, I've met a few significant individuals who have truly moved me. One of my heroes is a survivor of more difficult circumstances than I will ever face. Her name is Trisha Meili, better known to the world as the Central Park Jogger.[20]

Trisha's story speaks to the power of support in healing. On April 19, 1989, as reported in the press worldwide, Trisha went for a run after work in New York's Central Park. She was attacked by a group of young men, bound and gagged, raped, beaten, and left for dead. Hours later, she was found in a coma by passersby, having lost seventy-five percent of her blood. Trisha had suffered traumatic injuries, leaving her with severe physical and cognitive dysfunction.

Given four of a possible fifteen points on the Glasgow Coma Scale (one earns three points for simply being alive), Tricia stayed in a deep coma for twelve days. A hidden blessing rests in the fact that she has no memory of the brutal attack because of her brain injury.

The incident elicited a collective gasp of shock as we thought about the brutality of the attack and its implications about our modern society. The term *wilding* came into our vernacular to describe the behavior of the group of young men who terrorized and attacked several innocent people that evening, and who ultimately chose Trisha as one of their victims.

At least two miracles resulted from Trisha's ordeal. First, she survived. Beyond the expectations of her medical team, she fought a long battle to regain her physical and mental abilities. She spent nearly two months in New York's Metropolitan Hospital and then over five months at Gaylord Hospital in Wallingford, Connecticut, for rehabilitation.

The second miracle is that she touched the hearts of millions, resulting in an outpouring of love, support, and prayer. People wanted to let Trisha know that society's savagery came from only a few, as the vast majority extended their hearts to her and let her know they cared. Complete strangers from all over the world sent cards, letters, gifts, poems, healing oils, and holy water. Frank Sinatra sent eighteen roses.

Months after the attack, a man ran the New York City Marathon in Trisha's honor. The next day he shipped his medal to her at Gaylord Hospital with a note that read, "This is for you as you come closer to finishing your own marathon." As a runner herself, Trisha knew that it took months of training to prepare for the marathon. His gift represented many hours of dedicated work, and it meant the world to her.[21]

The Power to Heal

These demonstrations of support were confirmation that Trisha wasn't alone in her struggle to recover and heal. Why is support so critically important? She had come to understand there is a spirit deep inside of us that can help us heal, and it is the support of others that brings that spirit alive and unleashes a resource we all have, the power to heal. One lesson for all of us is that we can be part of the healing process of others by reaching out to them.

Another source of support for Trisha's recovery came from her employer, Salomon Brothers (now a part of Citigroup Global Markets), where she had served as an investment banker. Salomon Brothers stood by Trisha through her entire recovery, promising a job when she was ready to return. They even installed a work cubicle in her room at Gaylord, including a desk, telephone, computer, printer, and filing cabinet. The company even hung a small sign with their logo that read "Connecticut Branch."

The message from Salomon Brothers was that Trisha had a place to go back to, a step toward returning to normalcy in her life. Her employers were responding from their collective hearts—a crystal clear demonstration of the power that organizations can wield in healing support of their employees when they are driven by compassion as well as profit.

Be Proud of What You Have

Trisha shares her message of recovery in mind, body, and spirit with groups everywhere as a part of her own ongoing healing. She finds it to be a satisfying way to serve others and give support. She also shares two other lessons in her frequent speeches. The first: Be proud of what you can accomplish rather than focusing on what you can't.

Prior to the attack, Trisha had earned a graduate degree in business and international relations from Yale and, before that, an undergraduate degree from Wellesley, where she made Phi Beta Kappa her junior year. She was also a marathon runner, so she was accustomed to incredible achievements in every aspect of her life. At Gaylord, Trisha's first run was a slow walk for one-quarter of a mile around the parking lot. Given what she had been through, it was a huge accomplishment.

There is no value in looking back at what we used to have but have lost. Especially after significant suffering in our lives, healing comes from appreciation of what we have, not from what we have lost. Feeling good about what we CAN accomplish leads to more progress.

The Present Moment

The second lesson is the power of the present moment. Trisha became whole again when she realized she could not change her past and that paying attention in the present moment is all that matters. Holding onto anger and regret about the past or worrying about the future doesn't make any difference. The only way to impact the future is to focus on what can be accomplished right now.

Because of Trisha's brain trauma she lost the use of her hands. An exercise she used during her rehabilitation to improve her manual dexterity was called "put the nail in the hole." Her physical therapist at Gaylord presented her with a small board containing several drilled holes. Some of the holes had nails in them and some were open. Her task was to move as many nails as possible with tweezers into the open holes. Trisha performed the challenge over and over again, first with her right hand, then with her left.

This task might seem simple to us, but for Trisha it required intense concentration and patience. After being a marathon runner and earning an MBA from Yale, one could imagine that it would be easy to become frustrated and give up. But Trisha didn't. She focused on the moment, improving her ability to move nails on the board, not worrying about the future, just moving nails. Wallowing in the past was not going to help. Working in the present moment was what she could control.

In November of 1995, more than six years after her attack, Trisha demonstrated the incredible power of support and her own dedication to her healing by running the New York City Marathon. Her journey back had begun by walking one-quarter of a mile at Gaylord Hospital. After nearly losing her life, after doctors had predicted that she would never regain her physical or mental capabilities, Trisha defied the odds by running the 26.2 miles in four and one-half hours.

She recounts the last few miles of the marathon, running through Central Park, once again feeling the support of strangers who were cheering on the sidelines. She had come back to attest to the power of healing, to celebrate her accomplishments, and to reclaim her park.

Trisha is a modern-day Viktor Frankl, teaching us all once again that, no matter the challenges or the obstacles and with the right support from others, we can accomplish incredible things. We face challenges in our lives, and it is easy to believe that when it hurts we are supposed to give up, to give in to the hurt. It is the support of others that reminds us we always have a choice.

We forget about the importance of support in our lives until we are reminded of its power by the example of someone like Trisha Meili or from reaching our own crisis point. Often those "tipping points" in our own lives show us that we need each other to navigate through a life full of land mines and unexpected life events.

We need support to do the really hard things in life. Personal balance is one of those really hard things. So why do we shy away from asking for support from others?

...

"You alone can do it,
but you cannot do it alone."
– O. Hobbart Mowrer

...

Individualism

In 1831, Alexis de Tocqueville visited the United States from his native France and eventually wrote a two-volume book to share his observations, which he entitled *Democracy in America*.[22] In one of the most quoted books about life in the early U.S., de Tocqueville described the characteristics he noticed in the citizens of our country almost two hundred years ago.

One of the most distinctive traits of early Americans he described is *individualism*. De Tocqueville found a people who showed both creativity and determination to succeed in challenging circumstances. American ingenuity had already found its way here, born out of the necessity to survive on the frontier. Early Americans did what they had to do to get by.

If one reflects on individualism—believing in and valuing independent thought and action—it's not surprising that those who lived here in the early 1800s scored high in this trait. The early immigrants came here to escape the caste system that had trapped them economically in their old countries or to escape the many forms of social and religious persecution that had held them prisoners of their past. One would have to be highly driven to take the risk of moving to a new continent, a long and treacherous journey, to face a new world of hope but little security.

Those were the people who came to America. The risk-averse and dependent stayed home, and the independent struck out on a new adventure.

The early settlers were a reflection of the times and of the kinds of people who were able to survive in the wilderness. If a wagon wheel fell off or broke in two, the wagon master had better find a way to repair it or build another, or the wagon train was stopped. If survival depended on immediate medical care, one had better find a way to get healthy. The ability to survive and get by on one's own wits became a requirement, and it also became a quality of the culture.

I remember my dad thawing out frozen underground pipes in the dead of winter to get water to the cows in the barn on our southwestern Michigan farm. There was no one else to do it. When the tractor broke down, he figured out how to fix it or to get a neighbor who could help, as there wasn't money to pay a mechanic. In Dad's time, Barry County, Michigan, was full of people just like him who did everything for themselves, from building their own houses to growing their own food.

I remember my mom somehow finding a way to raise eight infants into childhood using cloth diapers. With the help of the older kids, she washed all of our clothes with a "ringer-washer." The laundry then had to be hung outdoors on a clothesline to dry. All of us kids helped her tend a huge garden that we relied on as much as our chickens and cattle for food. She worked every night canning our vegetables, mending clothes, or darning socks to keep us fed and clothed.

Mom chased a cow or a pony when the fence broke and fixed it herself if my dad was not around. We didn't go to the emergency room at the hospital unless we really needed to, as our mom became the family doctor when necessary.

For my mom and dad, theirs was a code that country people clung to. And this was 130 years after Alexis de Tocqueville made his observations about early Americans. In 1830, over ninety-one percent of people in the United States lived in a rural setting. Individualism in political thought as well as in practical action was required for survival.

Rugged Individualism

Individualism emerged as a cultural value in America, a trait that we as a country admired in the day and still do. Individualism as a value morphed into *rugged individualism*, a belief that nearly all individuals can succeed on their own, a belief in personal liberty, and a belief in self-reliance. These are values that are core to our heritage.

An unfortunate aspect of rugged individualism is the often unspoken perception that asking for support from others is a *weakness*, an indication that someone is not strong enough to make it on his own. When rugged individualism becomes a core value, requesting support from others can be seen as a failure. Our schools often teach in subtle ways, over and over again, that success is predicated on an ability to "work on your own," even in the face of research that demonstrates cooperative learning as superior.

With these beliefs in mind, either conscious or unconscious, we learn to develop another façade: "I have no weakness, and I don't need anyone's help!" We become emotionally uncomfortable accepting support from others. In the Western culture, beer commercials that teach us to mimic "I love you, man" reinforce our common conspiracy to show genuine emotion and support for only our closest relationships.

We struggle on in quiet frustration until we experience a crisis and can't hold up the façade any longer. Until the fact that we need each other for support to get through this life won't stay hidden any longer. Why do we wait until an emotionally significant loss or a crisis to reach out to one another?

We Need Support

Successful people and organizations need individualism as well as collaboration. We need to accept personal accountability for the results we create. We need to stand on our own, to leave whatever nest keeps us dependent, to walk our own paths. We need to shed the *rugged* part of individualism, the unwillingness to show any weakness or imperfection. We can try to hide it, but we are imperfect human beings, and we really need one another.

Rugged individualism leads to pretense: "I have no faults or shortcomings." We often support a conspiracy with each other that sounds like this: "Let's pretend that we are all strong and right!" In order to grow, we have to admit we are fallible human beings and are willing to accept support from others.

We hesitate to give others support when we are focused on our own agendas, and we especially avoid asking for that support. None of us would be successful in our lives without the support of others, and yet we are hesitant to ask for it when we need it to succeed.

Like any other developmental journey, achieving and especially maintaining personal balance requires the right support from others. It can come from coworkers, a boss, friends, family, loved ones, a personal trainer, a counselor, a coach, or from a variety of persons, but we will inevitably need support to succeed in the long term.

The kind of support we tend to give each other reinforces our victim mindsets: "It's too cold outside to go for a walk!" or "It's impossible to get up that early to go to the gym!" There is a somewhat cynical brand of humor made famous by Dilbert™ cartoons that is alive and well in corporate America. We like to strengthen each other's pessimism about the future: "This company is headed down the tubes, for sure!"

We support each other in all of the wrong mindsets and habits. We readily accept and support victim comments from each other: "That idiot was driving like an old lady in the left lane—I had to give him a piece of my mind! Who is going to teach him a lesson if I don't?"

What we need is support from others who understand both personal responsibility and the value in creating personal balance in our lives, not compounding our dysfunctional coping responses. We need people in our lives who encourage us to create good habits in mind, body, and spirit, and to help us change the game. Getting the right support also requires letting go of whatever gets in the way of asking, whether it is our egos, our pride, or our rugged individualism.

The challenge is to decide who can provide that kind of support for you, then to be willing to ask, and be willing to give, too. Perhaps that support can come from someone in your personal life, but it could also come from someone on your work team. Creating a culture of positive support for one another can create mutually positive energy in the workplace. We clearly do our very best work when we are living and working in positive and supportive environments.

The trick is to make a conscious decision about what support you will need and engineer it—to make sure it happens.

Support Tools and Techniques

Here is a list of ideas and tools that you might use to find support from others in achieving more personal balance in your life:

1. <u>Find a Balance Buddy</u>: Find someone who is willing to be your guardian angel—who will look out for you over the next year and act as your conscience. A real balance buddy cares about you and is someone who is truly committed to your success in bringing more balance to your life. He or she is willing to hold the mirror up to you, to use tough love if needed to keep you on track. A good balance buddy is someone with whom you can talk openly and who will in turn talk openly with you, especially when you need it.

2. <u>Create a Support Group</u>: Maybe a small group of balance buddies would work for you—a small support group to keep you on track. Weight Watchers has used this principle very successfully, as have many twelve-step groups fighting addictions together. The point is to be accountable to others, a strong motivator in any endeavor.

3. <u>Be Honest About Your Weaknesses</u>: Predict ahead of time when you will fall off the balance wagon and structure your

environment to avoid loss of momentum. If you struggle to get up in the morning, schedule an early time with a personal trainer and promise not to skip your workout. ("Hurt me, Helga!") Ask your significant other to post a chart of your progress on the refrigerator and help you stay on your diet. Ask your boss to help get you out of the office at 7 PM, and give her permission to request that you leave. Make a public commitment to your work team to stay calm in meetings and ask for their feedback.

4. <u>Keep a Log</u>: Write things down, including your goals, your commitments, your positive affirmations, and your progress. Keep an Excel table of data and a chart that measures your progress on your computer desktop so you see it every day.

5. <u>Publicly Post Commitments</u>: Write out your life vision and your balance goal on a note card and post it above your desk, so you keep your vision for balance in front of you. Maybe you could make your commitment your screen saver.

6. <u>Teach Others</u>: Sharing your knowledge with others reinforces your public commitment to balance and the support of others. Teaching can strengthen commitment and is a great reminder of the things that you already know you need to do.

7. <u>Get On Your Knees</u>: Give up control to a higher power and then listen for the guidance that will come your way.

"In the human world abundance does not happen automatically. It is created when we have the sense to choose community."

—Parker J. Palmer

Application and Notes

Take some time to write your thoughts about the support you will need to be successful with your personal balance plan:

1. Who will you need support from to be successful in finding more personal balance?

2. Specifically, what support will you ask for?

3. In turn, who could you support to achieve personal balance? How?

Notes:

CHAPTER 11

I Am!

"The privilege of a lifetime is being who you are."

—Joseph Campbell

Stand in front of a mirror and repeat the following question and answer three times:

Who is responsible for my personal balance? *I am!*

Finding personal balance in our lives begins with acceptance of personal accountability. Waiting for the world to change, for life to slow down, for life to get easier, is a fool's dream. It just won't happen. We have to reach out and take balance. If we don't, no one else will do it for us.

...

"Changing the universe is an inside job."
- David Bohm

...

The challenge, of course, is that we are ultimately responsible. We can't do it alone, and yet we have to do it by ourselves. The fact that it *is* our choice makes it hard but is also freeing. While it is easier to just keep going along, we can change if we want to.

The Levels of Commitment

It's really important to be honest with ourselves about the "want to" part. If we don't want to, fine. That's okay. We beat ourselves up enough already, and the rest of the world piles on, too.

Finding personal balance, finding true peace of mind as we negotiate this life, will most likely not happen accidentally or by default. Most of us can't escape to join a monastery or some other religious order, or we don't want to, so we need to find a way to get more peace in our lives while we keep our day jobs. A lot of us will be working *more* in the next few years. We will have to do it on the fly.

That is why commitment is so critical.

The ultimate test of commitment is the results that we get in our lives. If not committed, you will have a perfectly rational reason for not being successful. There just won't be enough time, or enough resources, or enough authority at work, or "Who really wants to get up that early to take a walk, anyway?" But if you are truly committed, you will find the time, and the resources, and the authority. You will take that walk. You'll take time to meditate on your lunch break if you need more sleep in the morning. If you are committed you will find a way, like the many who already do.

A friend saw this sign hanging in Boston: "Someone who is much busier than you is out for a run right now!"

Following is a "levels of commitment" scale so that you can determine where you are today. It is okay not to be committed; it is just important to be honest and to understand where you are.

Level 1: Resistance

- I am in opposition to an idea and I let others know.
- My thoughts of opposition to the idea are both covert (self-talk) and overt.
- I speak with conviction and passion about my resistance.

Level 2: Neutrality

- I do not feel compelled to take any position.
- I am comfortable changing my opinion based on the circumstances or my mood.
- I have no ownership of an idea or a position.
- I have equal levels of intellectual and emotional energy for any position.

Level 3: Compliance

- I do find merit in the ideas and the desired results.
- I am willing to express understanding and interest.
- I do not yet have ownership of the ideas.
- I will not personally initiate actions that lead to results.

Level 4: Support

- I will try hard to get the results I want.
- I will be engaged and take actions to get results.
- I do not have one hundred percent ownership of the results.
- I do not have sufficient control over my circumstances, and others are ultimately responsible.

Level 5: True Commitment

- I will do whatever is required, within my ethical and moral standards, to create the desired results.

- I will use my creativity and personal courage to deal with the expected obstacles as they arise.
- I have one hundred percent ownership of the results.
- I tell others about my commitment to the idea and the results.
- I speak with passion and conviction about my commitment.

Where are you? What would it take to get you truly committed?

If you want to find personal balance in this crazy world, you will need to be ready to commit and to take some action.

Your true self will be waiting inside for you when you are ready to start your personal journey toward health in mind, body, and spirit. Your true self is always there. Find it.

"Whatever you can do or dream you can, begin it!
Boldness has genius, power and magic in it."

—Goethe

Application and Notes

Take a moment to write down the commitments you are willing to make to your personal balance plan:

I commit to:

Notes:

Some Reading for a Spiritual Journey

Ready to start or reignite your own spiritual journey, or continue along the path? I am not a theologian or by any means an expert in spiritual growth or religion, but here are some of the books that have stimulated my own personal journey. Perhaps there is something here for you, a book with a message for you, a lesson that you are waiting to receive.

Here are my favorites:

M. Scott Peck, M.D., *The Road Less Traveled: A New Psychology of Love, Traditional Values, and Spiritual Growth* (New York, NY: A Touchstone Book published by Simon & Schuster, 1978).

M. Scott Peck, M.D., *The Different Drum: Community Making and Peace* (New York, NY: A Touchstone Book, published by Simon & Schuster, Inc., 1987).

Brian L. Weiss, M.D., *Many Lives, Many Masters: The True Story of a Prominent Psychologist, His Young Patient, and the Past Life Therapy That Changed Both Their Lives* (New York, NY: A Fireside Book, published by Simon & Schuster, 1988).

Brian L. Weiss, M.D., *Messages from the Masters: Tapping into the Power of Love* (New York, NY: Warner Books, published by Time Warner Book Group, 2000).

Marianne Williamson, *A Return To Love: Reflections on the Principles of "A Course in Miracles"* (New York, NY: HarperCollins Publishers, Inc., 1992).

Brennan Manning, *Ruthless Trust: The Ragamuffin's Path to God* (New York, NY: HarperCollins Publishers, Inc., 2000).

Oriah Mountain Dreamer, *The Dance: Moving to the Rhythms of Your True Self* (New York, NY: HarperCollins Publishers, Inc., 2001).

Deepak Chopra, *The Seven Spiritual Laws of Success: A Practical Guide to the Fulfillment of Your Dreams* (San Rafael, CA: Amber-Allen Publishing, 1994).

James Redfield, *The Celestine Prophecy: An Adventure* (New York, NY: Warner Books, Inc. published by A Time Warner Company, 1993).

Betty J. Eadie, *Embraced by the Light* (Placerville, CA: Gold Leaf Press, 1992).

Shunryu Suzuki, *Zen Mind, Beginner's Mind: Informal talks on Zen Meditation and Practice* (New York, NY: Weatherhill, Inc., 1995).

Pema Chödrön, *When Things Fall Apart: Heart Advice for Difficult Times* (Boston, MA: Shambala Publications, Inc., 1997).

Wayne W. Dyer, *There's A Spiritual Solution to Every Problem* (New York, NY: HarperCollins Publishers, Inc., 2001).

Wayne W. Dyer, *Getting In The Gap: Making Conscious Contact with God Through Meditation* (Carlsbad, CA: Hay House Inc., 2003).

Wayne W. Dyer, *Change Your Thoughts—Change Your Life: Living the Wisdom of the Tao* (Carlsbad, CA: Hay House Inc., 2007).

Bill Harris, *Thresholds of the Mind: Your Personal Roadmap to Success, Happiness, and Contentment* (Beaverton, OR: Centerpointe Press, Centerpointe Research Institute, 2007).

The Bible

Add your own books to this list and pass it along to someone you care about.

Bibliography

Barker, Joel A. *Paradigms: The Business of Discovering the Future.* New York: HarperCollins Publishers, Inc., 1993

Belloc, Nedra B. and Lester Breslow. "Relationship of Physical Health Status and Health Practices." *Preventative Medicine,* August, 1972.

Belloc, Nedra B. and Lester Breslow. "Relationship of Health Practices and Mortality." *Preventative Medicine,* March, 1973.

De Tocqueville, Alexis, Harvey C. Mansfield, and Delba Winthrop. *Democracy in America.* Chicago: University of Chicago Press, 2000.

Ellis, James and Esther Ellis. *LaGrange Pioneers.* Walworth County: LaGrange Ladies Aid Society, 1935.

Frankl, Viktor E. *Man's Search for Meaning.* Boston: Beacon Press, 2000.

Goleman, Daniel. *Emotional Intelligence: Why It Can Matter More Than IQ.* New York: Bantam Books, 1995.

Greene, Bob. *The Best Life Diet.* New York: Simon & Schuster, 2006.

Gupta, Sanjay. *Chasing Life: New Discoveries in the Search for Immortality to Help You Age Less Today.* New York: Warner Books Inc., 2007.

Harris, Bill. *Thresholds of the Mind: Your Personal Roadmap to Success, Happiness, and Contentment.* Beaverton: Centerpointe Press, Centerpointe Research Institute, 2007.

Hoffer, Richard. "Because It's Still There." *Sports Illustrated,* April 14, 2003.

Kuhn, Thomas S. *The Structure of Scientific Revolutions.* Chicago: University of Chicago Press, 1962.

Meili, Trisha. *I Am the Central Park Jogger: A Story of Hope and Possibility.* New York: Scribner, 2004.

Peck, M. Scott. *The Road Less Traveled: A New Psychology of Love, Traditional Values, and Spiritual Growth.* New York: Simon & Schuster, 1978.

Senge, Peter M. *The Fifth Discipline: The Art & Practice of the Learning Organization.* New York: Currency Doubleday, 1990.

The Surgeon General's Report on Nutrition and Health. U.S. Department of Health and Human Services, 1998.

Wilson, Larry and Hersch Wilson. *Play to Win.* Austin: Bard Press, Inc., 1998.

Notes

1. James Ellis and Esther Ellis, *LaGrange Pioneers* (Walworth County, Wisconsin: LaGrange Ladies Aid Society, 1935).

2. Larry Wilson and Hersch Wilson, *Play To Win* (Austin: Bard Press, Inc., 1998), 49–61.

3. My thanks to Larry Wilson for this story and many of the ideas here originally described in his "Results Model."

4. Viktor E. Frankl, *Man's Search for Meaning* (Boston: Beacon Press, 2000), 26.

5. Ibid., 86.

6. Thomas S. Kuhn, *The Structure of Scientific Revolutions* (Chicago: University of Chicago Press, 1962).

7. Joel A. Barker, *Paradigms: The Business of Discovering the Future* (New York: HarperCollins Publishers, Inc., 1993).

8. Peter M. Senge, *The Fifth Discipline: The Art & Practice of The Learning Organization* (New York: Currency Doubleday, 1990), 8–9.

9. M. Scott Peck, *The Road Less Traveled: A New Psychology of Love, Traditional Values, and Spiritual Growth* (New York: Simon & Schuster, 1978), 44.

10. Larry Wilson and Hersch Wilson, Play to Win (Austin: Bard Press, Inc., 1998), 67—68.

11. Thanks to Patrick Edwards for letting me use his diet story.

12. Bill Harris, *Thresholds of the Mind: Your Personal Roadmap to Success, Happiness, and Contentment* (Beaverton: Centerpointe Press, Centerpointe Research Institute, 2007), 134—135.

13. I learned the Paths of Choice model from my good friend and colleague, Patrick Edwards.

14. Daniel Goleman, *Emotional Intelligence: Why It Can Matter More Than IQ* (New York: Bantam Books, 1995), 34.

15. Richard Hoffer, "Because It's Still There," *Sports Illustrated*, April 14, 2003, A4—5.

16. Nedra B. Belloc and Lester Breslow, "Relationship of Physical Health Status and Health Practices," *Preventative Medicine*, August, 1972, 1(3):409—421.

17. *The Surgeon General's Report on Nutrition and Health.* U.S. Department of Health and Human Services (Public Health Service), 1988.

18. Bob Greene, *The Best Life Diet* (New York: Simon & Schuster, 2006).

19. Sanjay Gupta, *Chasing Life: New Discoveries in the Search for Immortality to Help You Age Less Today* (New York: Warner Books Inc., 2007).

20. Trisha Meili, *I Am the Central Park Jogger: A Story of Hope and Possibility* (New York: Scribner, 2004).

21. This story is excerpted from a speech I heard Trisha give to a group at Plug Power on April 6, 2005. If you are interested in learning more about Trisha Meili, visit http://www.centralparkjogger.com/.

22. Alexis de Tocqueville, Harvey C. Mansfield, and Delba Winthrop, *Democracy in America* (Chicago: University of Chicago Press, 2000).